T&T CLARK STUDY GUIDES TO TH

Genesis: A Past for a People in Need of a Future

Series Editor

Adrian Curtis, University of Manchester, UK

Published in association with the Society for Old Testament Study

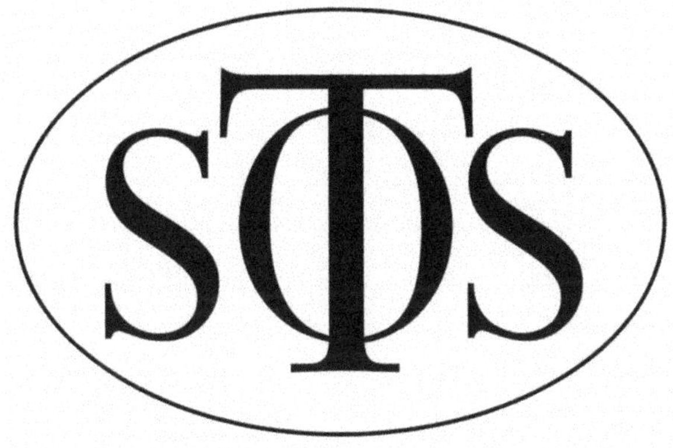

OTHER TITLES IN THE SERIES INCLUDE:

Amos: An Introduction and Study Guide

1 & 2 Kings: An Introduction and Study Guide

1 & 2 Samuel: An Introduction and Study Guide

Daniel: An Introduction and Study Guide

Ecclesiastes: An Introduction and Study Guide

Exodus: An Introduction and Study Guide

Ezra-Nehemiah: An Introduction and Study Guide

Haggai, Zechariah and Malachi: An Introduction and Study Guide

Isaiah: An Introduction and Study Guide

Jeremiah: An Introduction and Study Guide

Job: An Introduction and Study Guide

Joel, Obadiah, Habakkuk, Zephaniah: An Introduction and Study Guide

Joshua: An Introduction and Study Guide

Leviticus: An Introduction and Study Guide

Numbers: An Introduction and Study Guide

Proverbs: And Introduction and Study Guide

Psalms: An Introduction and Study Guide

Song of Songs: An Introduction and Study Guide

T & T CLARK STUDY GUIDES TO THE NEW TESTAMENT:

1 & 2 Thessalonians: An Introduction and Study Guide

1 Peter: An Introduction and Study Guide

2 Corinthians: An Introduction and Study Guide

Colossians: An Introduction and Study Guide

Ephesians: An Introduction and Study Guide

Galatians: An Introduction and Study Guide

Hebrews: An Introduction and Study Guide

James: An Introduction and Study Guide

John: An Introduction and Study Guide

Luke: An Introduction and Study Guide

Mark: An Introduction and Study Guide

Matthew: An Introduction and Study Guide
Philemon: An Introduction and Study Guide
Philippians: An Introduction and Study Guide
Romans: An Introduction and Study Guide
The Acts of the Apostles: An Introduction and Study Guide
The Letters of Jude and Second Peter: An Introduction and Study Guide

Genesis: A Past for a People in Need of a Future

An Introduction and Study Guide

Megan Warner

t&tclark
LONDON • NEW YORK • OXFORD • NEW DELHI • SYDNEY

T&T CLARK
Bloomsbury Publishing Plc
50 Bedford Square, London, WC1B 3DP, UK
1385 Broadway, New York, NY 10018, USA
29 Earlsfort Terrace, Dublin 2, Ireland

First published in Great Britain 2024

Cover design: Clare Turner

A catalogue record for this book is available from the British Library.

Library of Congress Cataloging-in-Publication Data
Names: Warner, Meg, author.
Title: Genesis: an introduction and study guide : a past for a people in need of a future / Megan Warner.
Description: London ; New York : T&T Clark, [2024] | Series: T&T Clark study guides to the Old Testament | Published in association with the Society for Old Testament Study. | Includes bibliographical references and index. |
Summary: "Introduces the Book of Genesis, examining its characteristics, historical context, and theological messaging, as well as its wider reception in literature, film, art and music"– Provided by publisher.
Identifiers: LCCN 2023008183 (print) | LCCN 2023008184 (ebook) |
ISBN 9780567693600 (hardback) | ISBN 9780567676641 (paperback) |
ISBN 9780567676658 (pdf) | ISBN 9780567676665 (epub)
Subjects: LCSH: Bible. Genesis–Criticism, interpretation, etc.
Classification: LCC BS1235.52 .W368 2024 (print) | LCC BS1235.52 (ebook) | DDC 222/.1106–dc23/eng/20230405
LC record available at https://lccn.loc.gov/2023008183
LC ebook record available at https://lccn.loc.gov/2023008184

ISBN: HB: 978-0-5676-9360-0
PB: 978-0-5676-7664-1
ePDF: 978-0-5676-7665-8
eBook: 978-0-5676-7666-5

Series: T&T Clark's Study Guides to the Old Testament

Typeset by Integra Software Services Pvt. Ltd.
Printed and bound in Great Britain

For Nina Valentine, with love and gratitude.

Contents

Series Preface

How can a potential reader be sure that a Guide to a biblical book is balanced and reliable? One answer is 'If the Guide has been produced under the auspices of an organisation such as the Society for Old Testament Study.'

Founded in 1917, the Society for Old Testament Study (or SOTS as it is commonly known) is a British and Irish society for Old Testament scholars, but with a world-wide membership. It seeks to foster the academic study of the Old Testament/Hebrew Bible in various ways, for example by arranging Conferences (usually twice per year) for its members, maintaining links with other learned societies with similar interests in the British Isles and abroad, and producing a range of publications, including scholarly monographs, and collections of essays by individual authors or on specific topics. Periodically, it has published volumes seeking to provide an overview of recent developments and emphases in the discipline at the time of publication. The annual Society for Old Testament Study Book List, containing succinct reviews by members of the Society of works on the Old Testament and related areas which have been published in the previous year or so, has proved an invaluable bibliographical resource.

With the needs of students in particular in mind, the Society also produced a series of Study Guides to the books of the Old Testament. This first series of Old Testament Guides, published for the Society by Sheffield Academic Press in the 1980s and 1990s, under the general editorship of the late Professor Norman Whybray, was well received as a very useful resource which teachers could recommend to their students with confidence. But it has inevitably become dated with the passage of time, hence the decision that a new series should be commissioned.

The aim of the new series is to continue the tradition established by the first Series, namely to provide a concise, comprehensive, manageable and affordable guide to each biblical book. The intention is that each volume will contain an authoritative overview of the current thinking on the traditional matters of Old Testament/Hebrew Bible introduction, addressing matters of content, major critical issues and theological perspectives, in the light of recent scholarship, and suggesting suitable further reading. Where appropriate to the particular biblical book or books, attention may also be given to less traditional approaches or particular theoretical perspectives.

All the authors are members of the Society, known for their scholarship and with wide experience of teaching in universities and colleges. The series general editor, Adrian Curtis, taught Old Testament/Hebrew Bible at the University of Manchester for many years, is a former Secretary of the Society, and was President of the Society for 2016.

It is the hope of the Society that these Guides will stimulate in their readers an appreciation of the body of literature whose study is at the heart of all its activities.

Author's Preface

Sometimes clarification of one's vague thoughts comes from the least likely sources. I have been working with the Book of Genesis for more than two decades, yet not one but two lightbulb moments came while on a recent long-haul flight to Australia, watching an in-flight movie. The movie was a German sci-fi rom-com (they don't make enough of those) called *Ich bin dein Mensch* ('I'm your man'). Fortunately for me, although the movie has nothing obviously to do with Genesis, it has just enough connection with the world of biblical studies – the heroine, Alma, is a cuneiform scholar, working at Berlin's Pergamon Museum (where it is possible to see a reconstruction of the Ishtar Gate that would have been seen also by the exiles) – for me almost to get away with writing about it here.

In the movie, Alma has been press-ganged by her boss into participating in an experiment looking at the potential for using artificial intelligence to build romantic life partners. Alma has no desire to participate in the experiment but agrees to trial a robot named Tom on the basis that she will be given funding to visit Boston to view a cuneiform collection. My first lightbulb moment came early in the movie, shortly after Alma and Tom are first introduced. Alma's boss sends the two of them off to have some initial conversation and, in particular, to come up with a story of how they met. When Alma expresses scepticism about inventing history, her boss explains that 'to have a future you need a past'. That truism became the central theme for this study guide to Genesis. Recent developments in dating of biblical texts, which place *at least* substantial amounts of the editing of Genesis in the post-exilic period, shine new light on the meaning and purpose of Genesis. It is becoming clearer that in the wake of the trauma of the destruction of Jerusalem, the disorientation of the exile, and the crushing disappointment of the eventual return, the Judahites needed a new identity story to propel them into a more hopeful future. The authors and editors of Genesis set about doing this through the writing of a 'new' history that was set sufficiently in the ancient past to introduce a whole new basis for relationship with Israel's God, Yahweh – one which could be understood not to have been tarnished and spoiled by Jerusalem's defeat at the hands of Babylon and the people's expulsion from the land. The Mosaic covenant may have been in tatters, but a whole new set of divine promises, made to ancestors who lived and died before Moses was born, could see the Israelites into the future.

The second lightbulb moment is related to the nature of the AI experiment in the film. At the core of the experiment was the question whether humans would respond well to life partners programmed to know and fulfil all of their deepest needs and desires. The answer offered by the film was a resounding 'no'. The humans who had spent any time in these relationships became flabby – gorged on instant gratification and unstimulated by the ordinary tensions of relationship. They took on the appearance of 'Stepford Wives' – happy but zombie-like. The message of the film, if there is one, is that humans require tension and conflict in relationship in order to build resilience and character. The message of Genesis, if there is 'one', could be understood to be pretty much the same. Genesis can be read as an extended case study of the tensions that arise in relationships – relationships between humans, between humans and God, and between humans, God and Earth. Genesis 1 presents a created world that is all 'good', but in Genesis 2 a problem presents itself. There is nobody to 'serve' Earth. When a human is created to resolve that problem, a new problem arises. The human requires a partner to assist in the work of the service of Earth. So God creates a second person. Once there are two people in the world, then suddenly there are enough problems between them to fill a whole book. The rest of Genesis is about the causes, and the roads to resolution, of these relationship problems. This focus on the tensions of relationship can be seen even in the name of God's chosen people, 'Israel'. This name is granted first to Jacob, who 'struggled' with God and with humans (Gen. 32:28). This focus on tension and conflict is a theme of Genesis that I have attempted to draw out in this study guide.

In writing this guide, I acknowledge my debt to John W. Rogerson, R.W.L. Moberly and William Johnstone (with John Goldingay), who did such valuable work in introducing Genesis (and Exodus) in the first series of these Old Testament Guides, while at the same time endeavouring to do justice to the fast-paced growth in our knowledge and understanding that has occurred in the two decades since. Their book was invaluable to me as a student (and also later as a teacher) and it is my sincere hope that this guide may help new generations of students to come to develop an understanding of, and a love for, Genesis.

Biblical translations are taken, unless indicated otherwise, from the NRSV, although transliteration of Hebrew divine names is adopted throughout (The LORD/Yahweh and God/Elohim).

Finally, I would like to express my thanks to my colleagues at Northern College and Luther King Centre for Theology and Ministry in Manchester – as fine a group of colleagues as anybody could wish for – and to Adrian Curtis, George J. Brooke and the staff at T&T Clark for their assistance and patience in the delivery of the manuscript for this study guide.

Megan Warner
Manchester
31 October 2022

Abbreviations

AIL	Ancient Israel and its Literature
BibInt	*Biblical Interpretation: A Journey of Contemporary Approaches*
BMW	The Bible in the Modern World
BZAW	Beihefte zur ZAW
CPREI	The Composition of the Pentateuch in Recent European Interpretation
FAT	Forschungen zum Alten Testament
HBM	Hebrew Bible Monographs
JBL	*Journal of Biblical Literature*
JSOT	*Journal for the Study of the Old Testament*
JSOTSup	*Journal for the Study of the Old Testament*, Supplement Series
OBO	Orbis biblicus et orientalis
OBT	Overtures to Biblical Theology
OT	Old Testament
OTR	Old Testament Readings
OTS	*Oudtestamentische Studiën*
SBL	Society of Biblical Literature
SBLRBS	SBL Resources for Biblical Study
SBLSS	SBL Semeia Studies
SBLSymp	SBL Symposium
SBT	Studies in Biblical Theology
TB	Trauma Bible

VT *Vetus Testamentum*

VTSup *Vetus Testamentum*, Supplements

WBC Word Biblical Commentary

1

What Is Genesis, Where Did It Come from, and Why?

It is common for books or commentaries about Genesis to open with a sentence that begins, 'Genesis is …'. It is, of course, either difficult or impossible to sum up Genesis in a single sentence. Nevertheless, I am going to risk giving it a shot, and say that Genesis is a curated collection of stories that furnished a people in need of a future with a past. If that sounds underwhelming – perhaps the Old Testament (OT) equivalent of offering a snake to a child who has asked for a fish (cf. Lk. 11:11) – it is not meant to. Without a past there can be no future. You need to know where you've come from in order to be able to write the story of your future. This is especially true for a population that has experienced disaster and found that the old stories, or the old past, no longer fit.

The first chapter of this study guide to Genesis delves into the questions asked in the chapter's title, as well as into the thinking behind this brief initial answer. In particular, it explores the genre and forms of Genesis, the history of its transmission (or the process by which Genesis became the book with which we're familiar) and the circumstances of Israel's history that gave rise to the need for such a book. Further chapters will consider the place of Genesis within the OT (Chapter 2), the themes and theology of Genesis (Chapter 3) and some of the more recent approaches that have been adopted for reading and interpreting Genesis (Chapter 4).

What Is Genesis?

Genesis has been identified and described in many different ways: for example, as a 'collection of stories', a 'study of beginnings', an 'exercise in identity building', an 'introduction', a 'prologue' and a 'prelude'. Attitudes to these kinds of labels or descriptors have changed over time. For example, Claus Westermann, writing in the late 1970s, argued that Gunkel's conception of Genesis as a 'collection of stories' was no longer adequate. Westermann pointed towards the careful framework elements of Genesis that knit it together as a coherent work, while also stressing the significant differences between different parts of Genesis that call for resistance to any overall description of Genesis as a whole. Nearly fifty years later, attitudes have shifted again, with scholars again embracing the recognition of a multiplicity or 'collection' of stories within Genesis (and eschewing notions of a single narrative or 'metanarrative'), while at the same time recognizing the various editorial hands that have worked to fashion these stories into a satisfying whole. Further, in recent years, commentators have increasingly tended to highlight the functionality of Genesis (i.e. what it *does* rather than what it *is*). Descriptions of Genesis as an exercise in identity-building have become common. Mark G. Brett, as a further example, has described Genesis as 'resistance literature' (Brett 2000), while I have explored elsewhere what it means to identify Genesis as 'resilience literature' (Warner 2023).

Any attempt to identify the genre(s) or form(s) of Genesis needs to take a variety of factors into consideration. Of course, the various internal elements that make up the book are important in this regard – one must enquire about the various types of literature that can be found within Genesis. Equally, however, it is instructive to consider external factors, such as Genesis' place and role in its literary context. What is the significance of the fact, for example, that Genesis comes first? And how do the larger groupings of biblical books to which Genesis may be considered to belong impact upon attempts to categorize it? I will address these external factors first, focusing on Genesis' literary context before zeroing in on its content.

Genesis has traditionally been understood to belong to a group of the first five books of the OT that has variously been termed 'Torah', 'Five Books of Moses' and 'Pentateuch'. One might think to look to these books, as a collection, for insight as to the genre or form of the individual books belonging to it. The Hebrew name 'Torah' is particularly suggestive. In English, 'Torah' is usually translated as 'law', although, strictly speaking, 'instruction' is a more accurate translation. The other four books of the Torah – Exodus, Leviticus, Numbers and Deuteronomy – all contain considerable amounts of law, held together within a narrative framework. When considered in the context of other Ancient Near East ('ANE') legal writings, this combination of law and narrative can be seen to be a highly distinctive, even unique, approach to the literary presentation of law collections. In fact, this distinctive combination – law and narrative – has been understood by some scholars to be the genre or form of those four books.

Genesis, however, is different from the rest of the Torah. Even though traditionally considered part of it, Genesis contains little or no material that could be categorized as law in the usual sense. In Genesis' own story-world there is no law – law does not appear in the biblical story until Moses receives it on Mt. Sinai (in the book of Exodus). Genesis is presented throughout as a depiction of a time before the law was known. (In fact, there are myriad clues throughout Genesis that its authors knew the Torah, and were writing with Torah very much in mind, but, with the exception of an extremely small number of explicit references, these same authors worked hard to ensure that no anomalous references to law made their way into Genesis' pages.) Genesis contains narrative, as the other four books do, but no law. Instead, the best-represented genre or form within Genesis, apart from narrative, is genealogy. Genealogy plays an extremely important role in Genesis, arguably providing the book's structural framework. Passages of genealogy are interspersed with passages of narrative, and the genealogy performs the function of organizing and connecting the series of accounts of the generations of the primary characters. The concept of 'generations' (*toledot* in Hebrew) is central to the structure and logic of the book, and a distinctive feature of Genesis is the use of the repeated motif 'These are the generations (*toledot*) of …'. The other type of material within Genesis that performs the function of structuring and punctuating the narrative can be described as 'promise' and 'blessing' material. Passages containing this material are used to overlay a consistent and coherent narrative arc upon the various generational stories collected together in Genesis. Structurally, however, it is the genealogical material in Genesis that has attracted most attention from scholars of Genesis, even causing some to suggest that the overall genre or form of Genesis could be said to be not 'law and narrative' (like the rest of the Torah) but 'genealogy and narrative'. I discuss the genealogical material and promise/blessing texts in more detail below when I focus on the content of Genesis.

A further external factor to be taken into account when assessing Genesis' genre or form is Genesis' position at the opening of the canon. Genesis may not have been written before the other books of the OT (see the discussion below), but it has been placed at their very beginning. Indeed, Genesis is a cosmological account of the beginning of God's creative activity, of the beginning of the history of Earth and her creatures, and of the earliest history of humankind, and this has been significant for many who have approached the question 'What is Genesis?' For example, the opening chapters of Genesis have been compared with the cosmological writings from elsewhere in the ANE, and the suggestion made that, as is the case for that literature, 'myth' is an appropriate genre label for at least some of Genesis, and most particularly Chapters 1–11 (often termed 'the Primeval History'). Again, 'myth' as genre label is addressed at greater length below.

A further way of thinking about Genesis' position at the opening of the OT is to consider its function. Scholars have suggested a range of genres or forms for Genesis that reflect its function as first book: these include 'prologue' (Van Seters, Römer, Schmid), 'prelude' (Carr), 'introduction' (Schmid), 'preface' (Moberly) and 'prequel' (Warner). Additionally, Walter Moberly's suggestion that Genesis can be thought of as 'The Old Testament of the Old Testament' (Moberly 1992) has been influential. Each of these suggested genres or forms points to the relationship between Genesis and the books that follow it, and the role played by Genesis in that relationship. In their discussions, each one of the scholars listed also reflects upon differences between Genesis and the books that follow it. These differences are not limited to the presence (or absence) of law. Scholars have noted substantial differences between Genesis and Exodus – Deuteronomy in a range of respects.

Genesis depicts a world that is in many ways quite distinct from that described in those other books. Genesis is a story of successive generations of families, or, arguably, of a single family. Its settings are overwhelmingly pastoral and agricultural. The religion reflected in its pages is unorganized and loosely defined. Relationships between the central characters and God are primarily mediated through blessings and promise. The political landscape is largely informal – overseen by a family-focused 'congregation' (*qahal* in Hebrew), although other 'nations' are represented as monarchical and land-owning. The overall tone of the book is relatively peaceful, even 'eirenic' (Habel 1993). Genesis is concerned with survival (of the central family and of humanity in general, but also of Earth) and with familial relationships, both within families and between families of different ethnic origins.

The world depicted in Exodus, Leviticus, Numbers and Deuteronomy differs in each one of these respects. These books tell a story of tribes coming together to form a nation. Although the tribes are depicted as being ambulatory and wilderness-based, their trajectory is towards settlement in a land of their own and city-based living. The religion reflected in their pages is Yahwhistic – painstakingly defined and dominated by the character of Moses. Relationship between the people and God is mediated through a conditional model of covenant. The political landscape is focused upon the corporate acquisition of land and sovereignty. The books imply an openness to, or even promotion of, the use of violence against other nations for the purpose of securing these ends. These four books are concerned with the future of a people, uniquely chosen by Yahweh, to be Yahweh's special nation.

Any assessment of what Genesis *is*, then, must engage with and account for the function of Genesis as part of its relationship with these other books (and with the other OT books that follow them), with which it manifestly belongs, but from which it equally manifestly differs. Descriptors or categories such as 'prologue', 'prelude', 'introduction', 'preface' and 'prequel' attempt to address both the relationship between Genesis and the other four books (and the function of Genesis within that relationship) and the differences between them.

The next stage in this exploration of what Genesis is, is to consider internal elements of Genesis. What kinds of text – or genres or forms – are to be found within Genesis? To some extent, this question has already been answered. Genesis contains a great deal of narrative, a lot of genealogy, some promise/blessing passages and some myth. To be sure, this is not an exhaustive list of the genres and forms to be found within Genesis. Genesis 1, for example, is not entirely narrative in form, and neither is it genealogy in any conventional sense. Genesis 1 has poetic and ritual elements that make it more like a litany than a narrative. Genesis 10, meanwhile, is, again, partly genealogical, but without conforming to typical patterns. It is often given the descriptor 'table of nations'. Genesis 49 also stands out. It comprises a long set of blessings, poetic in nature, spoken by a dying Jacob over his twelve sons. So, there are some unusual passages of text, but narrative and genealogy nevertheless comprise the bulk of the book.

Genealogy

Genealogy is used in Genesis to build a framework for the narrative, creating structure for the book and holding together the generational stories. As already noted, each section of genealogy is introduced by a variation on the formula 'These are the generations (*toledot*) of …'. This '*toledot* formula' appears ten times in Genesis (Gen. 2:4; 5:1; 6:9; 10:1; 11:10; 11:27; 25:12, 19; 36:1 (repeated in v. 9) and 37:2). The usage of the formula varies. Sometimes it appears prior to a section of genealogy and sometimes afterwards. Sometimes it introduces a recognizable list-based genealogy and sometimes it introduces a section of narrative. Usually, the formula introduces generations of people, but the very first instance of the formula introduces instead 'the generations of the heavens and the earth' (Gen. 2:4).

The structure supported by this use of *toledot* formula is illustrated in Table 1.1.

Table 1.1 Structure of Genesis.

	Genealogy	Narrative Cycle
Gen. 1–2:4a	The Heavens and the Earth	
Gen. 2:4b–11:9		Primeval History (including genealogies of Adam, Noah and Noah's sons)
Gen. 11:9-30	Shem (and Terah)	
Gen. 11:31–25:11		Abraham (including quasi-genealogical material in 22:20-24)
Gen. 25:12-18	Ishmael (and Isaac)	
Gen. 25:19–35:29		Jacob
Genesis 36	Esau (and sons of Esau)	
Genesis 37–50		Joseph

When set out in this way, several things can be observed about the structure of Genesis. First, it can be seen that the narrative is divided by genealogy into four major sections. The first of these, the Primeval History, occupies the first eleven chapters of the book. The second, running from Gen. 11:31 to 25:11, includes the narratives focused on Abraham. Isaac, the second member of the ancestral triad, doesn't have his own narrative block. Instead, Isaac material is to be found at the end of the Abraham section and beginning of the Jacob section. Jacob does receive his own section, which runs from Gen. 25:19 to 35:29. Finally, the fourth section, beginning at Genesis 37, is usually attributed to Joseph, although the genealogical notice in Gen. 37:2 reads, 'These are the generations of Jacob'. English translations of this verse tend to provide a gloss, to the effect that what follows is the story of the family of Jacob.

A second detail that can be seen in the table is that the Primeval History differs from the other three sections in that it contains a considerable amount of genealogical material within it. Indeed, the Primeval History is something of a microcosm of the rest of Genesis in that it includes within it substantial amounts of both narrative and genealogy. Set out in chiastic form, the Primeval History can be represented in this way:

Gen. 1-2:4 Introductory Genealogy (Heavens and the Earth)
Gen. 2:4-4 Tension between God and Humans (Eden, Cain and Abel), Civilization and separation (family)
Genesis 5 Genealogy (Adam)
Genesis 6-9 Tension between God, Humans and Earth: The Flood
Genesis 10 Genealogy (Noah's Sons)
Gen. 11:1-9 Tension between God and Humans: Babel, Civilization and separation (nations)
Gen. 11:10-30 Interstitial (i.e. in-between) Genealogy (Shem and Terah)

A very small amount of quasi-genealogical material can also be found within the Abraham, Jacob and Joseph sections, but it is minimal, so that the Primeval History is quite distinctive in this regard, as well as in numerous other ways.

A third thing that becomes apparent from Table 1.1 is that an important function of the genealogies is to fill in details of the lives and offspring of the minor (male) characters of Genesis – that is, those whose stories are not told at greater length in the narrative. The genealogies fill out the story, which, in the narrative, tends to be focused on the 'chosen' son in each generation.

Modern (and post-modern) readers have a tendency to be uninterested in genealogy, which can be experienced as dry and tedious in comparison with narrative, and many readers today are surprised when they discover that genealogy can play an important, revelatory and highly creative role in ancient literature. Recent studies have shown that a rich understanding of the role of genealogy is necessary for drawing the maximum amount of meaning from Genesis. One thing these studies have shown is that the genealogy in Genesis does not, for the most part, follow the model of its use in other ANE literature (Van Seters, Tobolowsky). Genealogy in the ANE developed from lists of kings and was developed for the accurate and efficient recording of monarchic history. Such lists were linear and shallow. They focused on each king and his son and heir. No record was made, for example, of a king's other sons or daughters. The genealogical style of Genesis, conversely, is influenced by the classical Greek model, which is strikingly different. Classical Greek genealogy is not linear and shallow but far more like a family tree, with an interest in the breadth of family structure – in kinship. Nor was classical Greek genealogy developed for the 'accurate' or 'efficient' recording of history. Rather, classical Greek genealogy was developed for storytelling and for the creative shaping, even inventing, of history to suit the interests and requirements of much later times. Tobolowsky (2017: 5), for example, writes:

> In short, while Babylonian king lists and oral genealogies suggest the capacity of lists to preserve data, the history of Greek myth genealogies suggests the opposite: the continued interest of literary actors, well after the periods genealogies describe, in manipulating them to serve contemporary ends and describe contemporary situations.

An appreciation of the adoption by the authors of Genesis of this model helps us to understand a great deal about Genesis and about the possible agendas of its authors. We know that those authors were writing centuries after the events being described in Genesis (see below for a more detailed discussion of Genesis' genesis). One of the creative possibilities offered by the use of genealogy is the joining together of previously disparate and independent narrative traditions, for reasons suiting the situation of the authors' own time, and Genesis scholars are increasingly open to the idea of this having occurred in the formation of Genesis. Recent European scholarship, in particular, is postulating a history of Genesis in which an older story of a northern hero (Jacob) was joined together with a newer story of a southern hero (Abraham) and linked by genealogy, with some additional narrative added to embroider the history of a proposed buffer or 'hinge' generation, embodied in the characters of Isaac, Rebekah and Ishmael. I will say more about this below, in a discussion of Genesis' transmission history, but I've said enough already to alert readers of Genesis to the need, and reward, for interest and suspicion when encountering genealogy.

Narrative

While narrative is, strictly speaking, too broad a category to count as a 'genre', it is nevertheless a handy category for gathering together various forms of prose that engage with story. Narrative appears in a variety of guises throughout Genesis. It has often been observed that narrative found in the Primeval History (Genesis 1–11) is different from that encountered in the Ancestral Narratives (Genesis 12–36), which is different again from the narrative in the Joseph Story (Genesis 37–50). The Primeval History is concerned with cosmological beginnings and in many respects its narrative shows the influence of the cosmological accounts of neighbouring nations, as already noted. Like those accounts, the narrative of the Primeval History has a feel of super-realism. It tells overblown and often apparently naive stories about the earliest days of Earth and her populations. Human characters live for impossible lengths of time and participate in paradigmatic situations and encounters that serve to illustrate and explain key facets of the relationships between God, Earth and humans, as well as plants, birds and animals. Although at certain points in the Primeval History the narrative focuses on single families, overwhelmingly its outlook is universalist (so that, for example, God is presented as creator of the entire world and not just of the nation of Israel). The universalism of the Primeval History can be contrasted with the particularism of Genesis 12–50, which follows the fortunes of a single family (itself representative of a single nation – Israel). Typically, and quite properly, the genre assigned to the narrative of the Primeval History is 'myth'. This should not be understood to mean that the narrative of the Primeval History is not true, but rather that it explores and represents truths and stories that are deeper and richer than those that can be conveyed through mere factual reportage, however accurate.

Narrative style and content change dramatically shortly before the opening of the Ancestral Narratives in Genesis 12. (These were referred to in the past as 'Patriarchal Narratives'. The newer language acknowledges the existence, and influence, of matriarchs along with patriarchs.) The story takes on a greater sense of realism, and becomes focused on a single family and its context. Although the storytelling varies in style and approach throughout the Ancestral Narratives, which (*pace* Gunkel) have something of a feel of a collection of stories, there is an overall sense of continuity and coherence, aided by a tendency towards the recurrence of events, situations or challenges across generations. Further, and as already implied, the narrative works on a number of levels simultaneously, so that the individual characters represent not only themselves but also the tribes or nations from which they come. So, for example, Abraham functions as a type of 'Israel', and Jacob is even given 'Israel' as a name. Ishmael represents the Arab tribes, while Esau represents Edom. This element is true also of the Joseph Story (with each of Jacob's sons or grandsons representing one of the Tribes of Israel) and, as a result, Genesis functions as both a familial and national story. It is not difficult, further, to perceive parallels between the concern of each new generation of Abraham's family to identify the 'chosen' son, and the preoccupation within a monarchic narrative with the identity of the child who will grow up to assume the throne. All of these factors and more have led some commentators to argue that the genre of Genesis

12–36 is 'history' or 'historical narrative'. There is certainly some validity to these arguments, although it should be remembered that even those books of the OT typically characterized as 'history' (especially by Christians), such as Samuel, Kings and Chronicles, are not the same kind of writings as those we would label 'history' today. Arguably, the Ancestral Narratives and books such as Kings and Chronicles are 'history' in a way analogous to the way in which the 'History Plays' of Shakespeare are history. Other possible genre labels for the Ancestral Narratives, such as 'family saga', acknowledge the storytelling element of the Ancestral Narratives without making implied claims for the accuracy of reportage that tends to be associated with 'history' or even 'historical narrative'.

New questions about genre and form arise when coming to what I am choosing to call the 'Joseph Story'. It has long been recognized that this extended tale differs in nature from that of the Ancestral Narratives that precede it. Whereas Genesis 12–36 strikes the reader as a gathered collection of smaller stories, leading the Abraham and Jacob collections to be referred to often as 'cycles', Genesis 37–50 has the feel of a longer, and more sustained, saga. Further, the techniques of historical criticism that have been at least partly successful in offering scholars insight into the composition and transmission histories of the Ancestral Narratives are generally accepted to be of little assistance when it comes to the Joseph Story. Genesis scholars have tended to be more comfortable with the notions of a single author and a unified composition when applied to the Joseph Story than in connection with other parts of Genesis. Yet even many of these same scholars seem, increasingly, to be proposing breaks, additions, and redactional layers within it, despite finding traditional source-critical theory mostly unhelpful. Currently, two primary proposals addressing the transmission history of the Joseph Story are competing for scholarly approval. It is necessary to mention them here because they have implications for the identification of form and genre. One model sees the Joseph Story as having existed and been circulated independently in the northern kingdom of Israel before being incorporated into Genesis. While proponents of this model are likely to disagree about the date of composition of this independent Joseph tradition, many would date it prior to the Babylonian exile, even if it were not incorporated into Genesis (in some form) until the post-exilic period. A second model sees the Joseph Story as having been composed only after the return from exile, by authors either situated outside Judah or having a particular interest in diasporic life (i.e. the life of Judahites lived outside Judah). For those who promote this model, 'diaspora novella' is seen as an appropriate descriptor, and thus the title 'Joseph Novella' is often used. The title I am using here, 'Joseph Story', seeks to distinguish the material in Genesis 37–50 both from the term 'cycle' (regularly used of the Abraham and Jacob materials) and from the term 'novella', lest I be taken to be making any particular proposals about the provenance of Genesis 37–50, or the pre-occupation of its author(s).

Promise and blessing material

Even if genealogy and narrative are the two principal genres or forms found in Genesis, I have already noted the presence of further material, found throughout the book. Passages dealing with divine promise and blessings can be found in all of Genesis' four major sections, usually situated within narrative. One of the reasons for singling it out is the finding of scholars (most notably Rolf Rendtorff) that Genesis' blessing and promise material is not embedded in the narrative very deeply. Instead, this material gives a sense of having been overlaid on the narrative, assisting genealogy in the task of knitting the four sections of Genesis, and the disparate and varying texts within them, into a single book. Although the promise and blessings made to Abraham and his descendants (and before him to some of the descendants of Adam) are not identical, they contain many similar elements and one of the effects is to help to build the impression of consistent and coherent narrative. This is despite the fact that the promise and blessing material doesn't always sit entirely comfortably with the material around it. For example, the insistence of Gen. 26:5 upon Abraham's fidelity to Torah is not consistently supported by data from the narratives in which Abraham appears. Indeed, some parts of the Abraham Cycle, such as the two Abraham 'wife-as-sister' stories in Gen. 12:10-20 and Genesis 20, seem remarkably concerned to expose Abraham's disregard for Torah. (All of this is further complicated, of course, by the fact that in Genesis' story-world there was no Torah.)

Tentative conclusions about genre and form

It will be apparent from this discussion that there is no easy answer to the question 'what is Genesis?' Neither the book as a whole nor its constituent parts, which differ from each other quite markedly, can be labelled easily or helpfully. Even the language of 'book' is not unproblematic and is used here only loosely. Pointers to genre and form found both within Genesis and external to it are sometimes helpful, but equally sometimes add to an already complicated picture. Genesis is Torah, and yet not. It is a consistent and coherent book, and yet not. It is a history of sorts, and yet not. Hendel (2012: 76) has argued that 'modern terms such as myth, legend, epic, and the like, while valuable analytically, are inexact categories to denote the genres and forms of Genesis'. Hendel suggests, instead, adopting Genesis' own term *toledot* as a 'native designation', although he notes that the *toledot* formula expresses what Genesis *does*, rather than what it *is*: 'it articulates a genealogical narrative from the birth of the cosmos to the birth and lives of the eponymous ancestors of the twelve tribes of Israel. It is a genealogy of the world, which moves towards the teleological focus of the genealogy, the people of Israel' (2012: 77). Other scholars, too, have abandoned traditional technical language when attempting to define what Genesis *is*, increasingly favouring looser expressions, such as 'story of beginnings' or 'identity-building exercise'.

I've begun with questions about genre and form because, despite the evasiveness and opacity of the answers offered here, the discussion has begun to open up associated questions about the structure of Genesis, its themes and concerns, and the story of its own genesis. It is to that latter issue that I now turn.

Where Did Genesis Come From?

In the introduction to his 1987 Genesis commentary, Gordon J. Wenham observed: 'Writing a commentary on Genesis is thus a particularly awkward assignment at the moment' (1987: xxxv). In the three-and-a-half decades since, the awkwardness has only increased, and in no aspect is that sentiment more apt than in relation to questions about the provenance of Genesis.

The problems are not unique to Genesis, of course. Pentateuchal scholarship has become exponentially more complicated in recent decades, and especially so around issues of dating, both relative and absolute, and transmission history. The difficulties reflect the collapse of points of consensus that kept pentateuchal scholarship relatively buoyant until, perhaps, the 1970s. Since that time, views and approaches have both diverged dramatically, and been subject to geographic trends, so that it has become possible to identify distinctive outlooks of three major interpretive centres: Israel, Europe and North America. During this time too, of course, biblical scholarship outside these centres has continued to grow and flourish, although in many of these parts of the world, historical-critical approaches have been de-privileged, or largely abandoned, in favour of other approaches that are seen to respond more directly to local needs, interests and issues of justice and culture. In Israel, Europe and North America, and among scholars influenced by these centres of scholarship, meanwhile, interest in historical critical approaches has remained, but grown more polarized. A 2016 volume of collected essays addressing the issues (Gertz et al. 2016) runs to just over 1200 pages. In their introduction to the volume, the editors write (2016: 3):

> In the three major centres of Research on the Pentateuch – North America, Israel and Europe – scholars tend to operate from such different premises, employ such divergent methods, and reach such inconsistent results that meaningful progress has become impossible. The models continue to proliferate but the communication seems only to diminish.

Nevertheless, there is a particular poignancy when it comes to addressing questions of dating and transmission of Genesis. This is because Genesis research was central to the development of the Newer Documentary Hypothesis in the first place. Thomas Römer (2006: 24), for example, writes that 'It is a well-known fact that the entire Documentary Hypothesis, including the notion of a Yahwistic document, was essentially elaborated through analyses of the book of Genesis'. It was within Genesis study that scholars became attuned to the questions raised by the text's employment of multiple divine names, abrupt changes in style, repetitions, inconsistencies and so on. Konrad Schmid (2018: 23) agrees with Römer, but goes further, arguing that the use of Genesis as a model for the rest of the Pentateuch was misguided, and seriously so:

> Pentateuchal scholarship, particularly in its beginnings in the 18th century, but also in its more recent phases, has been dominated by the analysis and evaluation of the book of Genesis. What had been concluded for Genesis was also deemed to be true for the subsequent books of the Pentateuch, even if the textual evidence did not support such a transfer of concepts. In fact, the extrapolation of the findings from the book of Genesis to the rest of the Pentateuch is one of the most serious flaws of Pentateuchal scholarship from Astruc up to the 1970s and even still today.

Perhaps the greatest irony in all of this is that analysis of Genesis has been central, too, to the near-collapse of the traditional Documentary

Hypothesis. For example, scholarship has become increasingly cognizant of the fact that attention to usage of (multiple) divine names within text (an early spur to source-critical theory) is not reliable as a guide to the identification of sources. Early conceptions of a Yahwist source that felt at liberty to use the name 'Yahweh' prior to its announcement to Moses in Exodus 3, and an Elohistic source that maintained a discipline of the use of 'Elohim' to that point (and therefore throughout Genesis), have been exposed as shaky, as commentators posit alternative reasons for divine name choice. There has been increased recognition that context likely plays a role in this regard, as theories about the likely familiarity, or lack thereof, of Israelites (Albertz, Schmid) and non-Israelites (Achenbach, Brett), with the divine name Yahweh proliferate, alongside more literary concerns, such as interest in the comparative willingness of authors to make divine names known to their readers and to the characters populating their narratives. By way of illustration of this final point, readers of Genesis 17 might note the use of both divine names, 'Yahweh' and 'Elohim', within the first verse. While classical theory might point to a conflation of sources, readers today are more likely to posit that an author wished readers to know that it was Yahweh who spoke to Abram, but to understand further that Abram knew his divine interlocutor only as 'Elohim'.

Perhaps the single most significant challenge to the documentary hypothesis, the so-called 'death of the Yahwist' theory, also centres on Genesis. Central to the documentary hypothesis had been the idea of a collection of 'long', intertwined, literary documents or sources that run (almost) the full length of the Pentateuch. This idea led eighteenth-century theorists to identify a Yahwist, an Elohist, a Priestly writer and a Deuteronomist (although the work of the latter was thought to be restricted almost entirely to Deuteronomy). The most serious challenge to the idea of long, intertwined sources has come from an argument that the Yahwist (or 'J', from the German 'Jahwist') source, which had initially been thought of as the earliest framework for the Pentateuch, does not extend from Genesis to Exodus. Interestingly, as Schmid has pointed out, some of the earliest proponents of the source critical approach had limited their identified 'J' and 'E' sources to Genesis alone, so this idea is not, strictly speaking, new but represents a direction not initially taken. A collection of essays published in English in 2006, written primarily although not exclusively by European authors and titled 'A Farewell to the Yahwist?', explores the implications of the possible lack of an early literary bridge between Genesis and Exodus. Konrad Schmid is best associated with the argument that 'P' and not 'J' represents the first joining together of disparate Genesis and Exodus traditions, and that this connection was likely not made until the Persian period (Schmid 2010). This argument, together with other considerations about the place of Genesis in its literary context, is explored in depth in Chapter 2 of this book.

The necessary implication of all these developments is that it is not possible, or wise, to offer a single answer to the (deliberately naive) question 'where did Genesis come from?'. Divergences in theory about the earliest origins of Genesis, as well as its transmission history, mean that any attempt to do so is likely to be dismissed out-of-hand by at least two-thirds of one's readers. The most helpful thing for the student of Genesis is to be offered some guidance as to the approaches to answering this question most likely to be taken in the three principal geographic centres of pentateuchal study.

Israel

Israel is perhaps the centre in which the Documentary Hypothesis, in one form or another, has continued to be most employed. Gertz and his fellow-editors of *The Formation of the Pentateuch* suggest (2016: 3) that scholars based particularly in Jerusalem 'see the future of pentateuchal scholarship in the refinement rather than the abandonment of the sources J, E, P and D for the reconstruction of the compositional history of the Pentateuch'. This arguably 'conservative' approach tends to be matched by a 'conservatism' in dating. Israeli scholars are far more likely than those in Europe to date material in Genesis, even that assigned to P, the latest of the sources recognized in Genesis, earlier than the exile. Israeli scholars are also less likely than European scholars to label text 'redactional' and, in particular, as 'post-Priestly'.

Some new developments in Israeli scholarship have, nevertheless, had a profound influence on scholarship in Europe and elsewhere. Among these are pioneering hypotheses about P, especially hypotheses identifying multiple layers of P, which is perhaps now better conceived of as a 'school' than a source. One of the most significant of these hypotheses concerns 'H', or the work of a 'Holiness School'. It has long been recognized that Chapters 17–26 of Leviticus have a special focus on holiness, but traditionally this portion of Leviticus was considered older than the remainder of the book. Israeli scholars, and in particular Israel Knohl, whose work was developed by Jacob Milgrom among others, argued that Leviticus 17–26 should be dated later than the earlier chapters of Leviticus and that they represented a later stage of Priestly writing, further examples of which could be found also in other books of the Pentateuch, including (to a lesser degree) Genesis (Knohl 1995). Although scholars in all three centres have been wary of identifying examples of H influence in Genesis, Milgrom suggested tentatively that Genesis 1 might be assigned to H and, further, that this might point to H as a possible compiler of the Pentateuch (Milgrom 2003). Other scholars have since, although often with some resistance, seen evidence of H in other Priestly texts in Genesis, including Genesis 23, and some, including myself, have argued for the influence of H in non-Priestly texts in Genesis. The implications of H scholarship have possibly been greater within European scholarship, which tends to favour later dating models, than within Israeli scholarship, which, as already mentioned, continues to favour models in which all four sources had their origins prior to the sixth-century destruction of Jerusalem. Milgrom even dated the early period of H prior to the exile, although he recognized a continuation of a school until at least the earlier parts of the post-return period.

North America

The North American picture is not dramatically different from that in Israel, although it is perhaps more varied. Like Israeli scholarship, Northern American scholarship tends to favour continued reliance upon the Newer Documentary Hypothesis, and relatively conservative, or early, dating proposals. There tends, further, to be a particularly strong focus among North American scholars upon the value of approaches that focus on the study of biblical precursors and extra-biblical material, and in particular ANE texts and Second Temple Literature.

One development within Northern American scholarship deserves particular mention. The 'New Documentarians' are a group of scholars based in the United States, although strongly influenced by the teaching of Baruch Schwartz. The best known representatives of this group are Joel Baden and Jeffrey Stackert. The approach of the group is to promote a return to the documentary hypothesis, albeit in refined form. The hypothesis of the New Documentarians is that the entire Pentateuch, including Genesis, can substantially be accounted for as the work of a single editor, who combined the four original sources, conserving as much text as possible. The group allows for a certain amount of redactional activity having occurred subsequent to the initial joining of the sources, but far less than that contemplated by European scholars. The New Documentarians appear to have attempted to position themselves as one side of a two-sided debate about the origins of the Pentateuch, with some success and influence within the United States, but far less outside it. It would certainly not be correct to argue that the approach of the New Documentarians has captured US scholarship, but the group is almost always represented in international gatherings, and scholarship within the United States often recognizes a necessity for response to its work.

One further scholar based in the United States deserves particular mention in relation to Pentateuchal historical criticism, and especially that regarding Genesis, on the strength of his monograph *Reading the Fractures of Genesis* (1996). David M. Carr has been able to forge and occupy a scholarly position that straddles, to some extent, the positions of the three geographic centres. Carr has demonstrated an openness to developments within European scholarship, while at the same time urging moderation, particularly in relation to dating proposals. On the one hand, Carr has agreed with European scholars that scholarship identifying an 'E' source should now be disregarded, and has supported a practice of distinguishing between 'P' and 'non-P' text, which avoids reference either to E or J. On the other hand, Carr is more likely than European scholars to argue that identifiably redactional and 'late' material within Genesis was added to its context *prior* to the combination of 'P' and 'non-P' sources. He has made this argument, for example, in respect of key Genesis texts, including Gen. 18:17-19; 22:15-18 and 26:3-5, texts that European scholars generally have little hesitancy labelling 'post-P'.

Europe

It is in European scholarship that the greatest developments away from traditional models have occurred, and some of these have already been hinted at above. It would not be correct to say that the Documentary Hypothesis has been abandoned in Europe, but European scholarship, prompted in large part by Rolf Rendtorff's *Das überlieferungsgeschichte Problem des Pentateuch*, published in 1977 (and translated into English in 1990), has moved in a very different direction. Rather than four extended sources within (and across) the Pentateuch, European scholarship now recognizes the existence of a multiplicity of discrete blocks (or fragments) of text that have been joined together. As Schmid has observed (2018), the incisions required to separate elements of text are not, within European scholarship, horizontal (as would be the case for parallel narrative threads) but vertical (between discrete blocks of tradition). What that means for Genesis is a recognition that Genesis comprises a series of tradition blocks – Primeval History, Ancestral Narratives (often further divided into Abraham and Jacob blocks) and Joseph tradition. Within these large blocks, scholars may recognize smaller tradition complexes, such as the Laban material in the Jacob Cycle or the Noah tradition within the Primeval History. As mooted above, this approach does not necessarily jettison the Documentary Hypothesis in its entirety. Even if the full suite of implications of the hypothesis, in their totality, have been rejected, insights gained from the Hypothesis may still prove to be of assistance when assessing material within a single block, where the influence of broadly Priestly and non-Priestly (perhaps Deuteronomistic) hands can still readily be observed.

This dramatic change of focus has led to a number of consequential developments, of which the following may be considered examples:

1 The two earlier sources, E and J, have been all but abandoned. Most European scholars now refer either to 'P' and 'non-P' or to 'P' and 'D' as two primary competing schools or traditions at work during the Persian period, which gathered together earlier narrative traditions, and whose work was eventually brought together as part of a single account of Israel's origins and identity. Within Genesis, a division between 'P' and 'D' is complicated, of course, because there is little obviously 'D' material to be found in Genesis, which shows no knowledge even of Moses and alludes to Moses' Torah almost exclusively by implication and allusion. On the other hand, throughout the OT reference to the ancestors is to be found mostly in Priestly material, and so the ancestral traditions have come to be overwhelmingly associated with P. Some scholars, influenced by the work of Van Seters and others, continue to identify a 'Yahwist', and to attribute material to a Yahwist source, but date that source much later than traditional treatments, to the period just prior to the exile.

2 Corresponding to the two tradition complexes P and D (or 'non-P'), it is possible to identify two independent and competing origins traditions within the Pentateuch – P's 'creation' tradition and D's 'exodus' tradition. Genesis is, of course, the primary source of the former, while it contains little trace of the latter. Some texts in Genesis have, however, been identified as relating to the exodus tradition. Parts of Genesis 15, for example, have been thought to be elements

of a project to join Genesis and Exodus together as part of a larger Pentateuchal or Hexateuchal entity (see the discussion in Chapter 2).

3 Issues have arisen about Genesis' place with, and membership of, larger groupings of books, such Pentateuch, Triteuch, Enneateauch etc. (see, again, the discussion in Chapter 2).
4 New problems and debates have arisen with regard to P. In addition to the recognition of multiple 'layers' of P, questions have developed about the extent of P (or where P ends), the character of P (whether P is best characterized as a source or as a redaction layer) and the function of P (whether P, in one or other of its guises, can be credited with large-scale editing of book complexes, such as a Triteuch or Pentateuch).

In European scholarship, Genesis and its constituent parts are likely to be dated later than would be the case for Israeli or North American scholars. Further, the structure of Genesis is likely to be seen as more fragmentary and disparate. There is more room for recognizing a multiplicity of provenances for Genesis material. For example, a European scholar typically feels freer than an Israeli or a North American scholar to hypothesize that Genesis' Abraham tradition is southern, while its Jacob and Joseph traditions originated in the North, or, alternatively, in diaspora.

In sum, it is no easier to say where Genesis came from (and when) than it is to say what Genesis is. Such questions can best be responded to by outlining the various approaches and hypotheses favoured by scholars working in different parts of the world, or out of different academic world views.

One of the implications of the above recent history of interpretation, with its focus on the differing approaches favoured by relatively discrete geographical centres of scholarship, is that the subjectivity of pentateuchal scholarship, which has always been an important factor, has been magnified. In theory, the author of a study guide like this one has, if she chooses, the luxury of maintaining a stance of objectivity in setting out a range of positions held by others. The more honest approach, even when setting out a range of interpretational models, is, I suspect, to own one's own background and biases. That is, accordingly, what I propose to do, albeit briefly, here. I am writing this study guide in England, which is at one and the same time Europe and not-Europe. I am writing for a British series and publisher, and anticipating a primarily British readership. England, as well as being, in some respects, part of Europe, is influenced to a high degree by thought and scholarship, as well as by popular culture, of the United States. Meanwhile,

I myself am not a native of the UK. I was born, grew up and completed my theological studies in Australia. However, for most of my Australian years I felt myself to be living in an English outpost. I grew up in the Anglican Church of Australia (part of the Church of England's Anglican Communion) and got my earliest impressions of the world outside Australia from the BBC. I have become a UK citizen, but my background means that I am at one and the same time English and not-English. The three biblical teachers who have had the greatest impact on me (all Australian) all studied in the United States, although two were also students in Germany and/or England for a period. Although this mixed background does not make it inevitable that I should be most influenced by one or other of the three geographical centres, my tendency is to privilege European scholarship, which I find either most persuasive or most energizing (I am not sure I can confidently tell the difference). I have little doubt that this tendency will make itself known in this study guide (and suspect it has done so already), no matter how much I might aim for 'objectivity'.

In the wake of that exercise in self-disclosure, I feel able to risk offering some background into European scholarship about the provenance of Genesis, further to the more general discussion of European views about the provenance of the Pentateuch set out above. European scholars tend to date the Jacob material as the earliest in Genesis, and to see its beginnings in the Northern Kingdom in the centuries immediately pre-dating the Babylonian exile. Jacob, many of these scholars argue, was a prominent (probably the most prominent) religious hero of the north, and the stories collected in the Jacob Cycle reflect early traditions that grew up there, while serving as something of a foundational charter for the north's claims to theological and political pre-eminence. In recent work, it has been argued that this northern material was combined in the south with stories of a less-prominent southern hero, Abraham, to form a proto-Genesis, either in the period immediately preceding the exile or thereafter. It has been argued that the combination of the two traditions, one northern and one southern, was an element of a southern project to write a 'Panisraelite' history, in which the literary and political priority of the north (the writing of materials which eventually became part of the biblical canon is thought to have commenced in the north before the south) was 'borrowed' by the south. The aim of this project, it has been argued, was simultaneously to establish a unified Israelite history, and claim southern superiority within it.

As part of the joining of these two tradition complexes, it is maintained, an Isaac tradition was created, largely building upon the Abraham materials.

It has often been observed that Isaac is an under-drawn character, who repeats the actions of his more-illustrious father. Meanwhile, the Joseph materials were added in such a way as to present Joseph and his brothers (the eponymous tribes of Israel), as sons of Jacob. Some scholars argue that the Joseph Story had its origins in the north before being 'borrowed', like the Jacob tradition, by southern scribes, as I suggested above. I have argued elsewhere, as have others, that southern editing that can readily be identified within Genesis 37–50 appears to de-prioritize the character of Joseph in favour of a character bearing the name of the south, Judah. Other scholars see the Joseph Story, in its entirety, as being a composition of the post-exilic period, and having a particular focus upon the concerns of diaspora life, as already indicated.

Finally, the Primeval History is now often seen as being among the latest of the Genesis texts, if not being the latest of the large blocks to have become part of proto-Genesis. European responses to the Primeval History played an important part in Europe's movement away from a source-based model, especially as European scholars began to argue that non-P text in Genesis 1–11 should be dated not earlier, but later, than P, turning traditional views on their head. This late dating of non-P material in the Primeval History presents a major challenge to ideas of a comprehensive non-P source (even encompassing Genesis as a whole, without considering Genesis/Exodus links) predating P, and even to the value of a source-based analysis of Genesis 1–11 at all.

Why Genesis?

The last section, which addressed European views about Genesis' provenance, began to consider possible purposes or agendas behind the creation of Genesis, at least from the point of view of European scholars. It is time to step back to consider the question 'why Genesis?' more generally.

Over recent decades, scholars have engaged with a theory, originally published by Peter Frei in German in the 1990s, about the motivations for, and factors influencing, the formation of the Pentateuch and its constituent books. According to Frei's theory of Persian imperial authorization, the Torah was both permitted and prompted in the post-exilic period by the Persian occupiers of Judah, who allowed and even encouraged their occupied territories to develop and promulgate their own local laws. Frei appealed to the models of other Persian-occupied territories, including Egypt, which apparently produced law collections in the closing years of the sixth century BCE, to argue that a similar process likely occurred in the Persian province of Yehud. This Persian sponsorship, according to the theory, will have encouraged a local effort to compile a kind of composite document holding together legal material from multiple schools of scribes, most notably those representing Priestly and Deuteronomistic outlooks.

For some years, Frei's theory attracted a great deal of support and was embraced as a neat explanation for many aspects of the Pentateuch. Many looked to Ezra 7 as helpful biblical evidence supporting Frei's thesis. Over time, however, Frei's theory, or at least its more dramatic elements, was subjected to intense critical attention. The core of Frei's theory has not been entirely rejected, however, and some scholars continue to embrace elements of the theory as explanation for the composite nature of the Pentateuch. Brett (2019: 112) suggests, 'These compromise theories … proceed more on the basis of inference to suggest that the political challenges of the time provide the best explanation for an archiving of competing traditions and, hence, for the complexities and contradictions within the Pentateuch as we have it.'

An additional complication, when it comes to Genesis, is that while Frei's theory has clear potential application for the rest of the Pentateuch, it does not obviously suggest a motive for the composition of Genesis, which uniquely does not serve as a vehicle for the promulgation of law. Why, in the context of responding to a Persian directive, or invitation, to compile a national lawbook, would Hebrew scribes have bothered with an entire book, comprised largely of origins stories, that closes prior to the birth of the prophet to whom the law was entrusted? Even if the core of Frei's theory holds good in generalities, we must look further in the case of Genesis.

The likely key, here, is the word 'origins'. Origins stories are stories of beginnings that are told for the purpose of building identity. Identity-building exercises, for both nations and individuals, are demanding and challenging. They tend not to be embarked upon simply for the sake of the exercise. Instead, they are begun during periods of great upheaval in the lives of nations and individuals, and generally following major crises that shake them to their roots. In the final chapter of this book, I explore one of the newer interpretive lenses for the reading of biblical literature – trauma theory. The use of trauma theory as lens has helped scholars to read biblical books, including Genesis, in new ways. In the coming years, Genesis will increasingly be read as literature that responds to the experience of major trauma by the people of Judah and Samaria. By way of example, in the brief Author's Preface to the first volume of her Genesis commentary, Kathleen O'Connor writes (2018: xv):

> For several years I set aside efforts on this Genesis commentary to complete a book about Jeremiah. The delay proved beneficial because my Jeremiah work gave me a surprising new lens with which to interpret Genesis; I had discovered trauma and disaster studies. To my astonishment, aspects of the national catastrophe so evident in that prophetic book – the fall of Judah and Jerusalem to the Babylonian Empire – left unmistakable traces across the book of Genesis and provided it with new urgency. The beautiful, perplexing, and astonishing accounts of the beginnings that make up Genesis serve the 'pastoral' purpose to help the people begin again in the face of the impossible.

Later, in the commentary proper, O'Connor has this to say about what her 'discovery' had shown her about Genesis (2018: 2–3):

> More than recording history, Genesis intervenes in history. It speaks of beginnings to incite hope among Israel's remnant that they too might begin again. The book offers a theology of beginnings to a people flattened by invasions, displacements, and the strong possibility that they will disappear among the prevailing empires. Its overarching purpose is to convince its audience that the Creator of the cosmos and of all that exists is recreating them now.

Although the use of trauma and disaster studies as interpretive lens is still in its infancy (albeit currently spreading in its influence at a great rate), O'Connor's perspective is by no means novel. Wenham's observation, in the opening pages of his own Genesis commentary, published a little over three decades previously, expresses a not-entirely unrelated sentiment (1987: xxii): 'The succession of catastrophes that befell humanity prior to Abraham's call show just why the election of Abraham and, in him, Israel, was necessary.' For more recent and detailed treatments, see Carr's *Holy Resilience* (2014) and my own *Effective Stories: Reading Genesis through the Lens of Resilience* (2023).

There may well be some irony, or paradox, behind the idea that what is necessary for the building of a future is a telling of the story of one's past. Nevertheless, this is the logic behind the bald assertion, in the opening sentences of this chapter, that Genesis furnishes a people in need of a future with a past. As Siri Hustvedt writes in her novel *The Summer without Men* (2011: 94), 'There is no future without a past, because what is to be cannot be imagined except as a form of repetition.' Genesis was needed, because against the backdrop of the Babylonian routing of Jerusalem, the exile of the literate populace of Jerusalem to Babylon and their eventual disheartening return to a still-decimated Jerusalem, it had become apparent to the returning scribes that repetition based on Judah's previous origins story was unlikely to presage a viable future.

Judah's previous 'origins story', the story of Mosaic Yahwism, had itself been developed during, and in response to the experiences of, the exile. It was a story that worked well for a people still in exile. It helped to answer some of the most excruciating questions that arose in the wake of Babylon's shock victory. Judah had previously experienced a series of attacks by armies from both Assyria and Babylon. These armies had had some successes, but had never managed to take Jerusalem itself. When Babylon was finally able to destroy Jerusalem and send its people into exile, every assumption that the Judahites had made about their God, and their relationship with their God, was fundamentally challenged. Israel was, after all, Yahweh's chosen people. Yahweh had previously been reliable as a God who had guaranteed victories for Yahweh's people. What had gone wrong this time? In the search for an answer to this core question, the exiles were faced with some unpalatable possible answers. Perhaps Yahweh was not, after all, the strong God that they had assumed Yahweh to be? Alternatively, if Yahweh really was strong, then was it possible that Yahweh was fickle, and had simply given up on Israel as a chosen people? The exiles found an answer that avoided both these unappealing options – Yahweh was neither weak nor fickle; rather, the failure was their own. They had not kept their end of the relationship bargain. The success of Babylon's attack was a sign not of the weakness or fickleness of Yahweh but rather of Yahweh's continuing fidelity and capacity to turn other nations into agents of punishment (and deliverance). In exile, Jerusalem's scribes developed (from fledgling ideas that can be seen already in Hosea and Amos) an origins story of divine relationship, mediated by a covenant that was conditional upon Israel's faithfulness to divine Torah. By this means, the shocking victory of the Babylonian army in Jerusalem could be explained – Judah had failed to keep her side of the bargain and so Yahweh had called in Babylon to administer the necessary punishment. The Pentateuch (or Hexateuch) became a vehicle for this theology, and for telling its associated origins story.

The biblical witness suggests that this story – this solution to the problem of Jerusalem's defeat – wasn't successful for long. The idea of defeat and exile, as punishment for Israel's failure to keep its end of the bargain by observing Yahweh's Torah, worked well in the short term. It reassured the exiled

Israelites that their God was strong and faithful, and that once Israel's time had been served, Yahweh would return them to Canaan. Once the return had happened, however, things must have looked rather different. For a start, the homecoming wasn't the glorious return that the exiles had spent decades imagining. The city walls and the temple hadn't been repaired, so they came back to a destroyed city. Further, Jerusalem was occupied by Persian forces and the longed-for re-establishment of the monarchy never eventuated. Biblical accounts from the period, what's more, point to arguments and tensions between various Israelite groups. Against this background, the picture of the future will have been disheartening. What would a future of covenant relationship with Yahweh look like if Israel continued to be poor at complying with the covenant's conditions? Could Israel expect a future in which she faced the regular need for punishment by military defeat and exile? Worse, might Israel's failures be so bad that Yahweh would eventually declare the covenant at an end? The story of Moses, covenant and Torah had been ideal for building hope for a return from exile in the short term, but in the longer term another, more forgiving, story was required.

Genesis, and the history of the ancestors, is that story. Genesis offered the Israelites new hope for a relationship with Yahweh, based not on a conditional covenant that had failed but on Yahweh's freely given promises and blessings. It told a story of promises made, and blessings given, before the Sinai covenant had been broken, or even handed down. It looked back to the past in order to build a future. Genesis is not free of covenant. To the contrary, covenant is central to the relationship between Yahweh and Yahweh's creation, including human beings, in Genesis. However, the covenants in Genesis (found in Genesis 9, 15 and 17) are not conditional *upon the observance of Torah*. Whether or not they are strictly *unconditional* has been a matter of debate, but they are not conditional in the same way that the Sinai covenant is conditional (see the further discussion in Chapter 3). The Priestly covenants in Genesis (Genesis 9 and 17) are even pronounced to be 'everlasting'. Similarly, Abraham and his heirs are chosen by Yahweh in Genesis, but they are not chosen in quite the same way that Israel is chosen in Mosaic Yahwism. Even the language is different – covenant passages in Genesis avoid the Hebrew root *bkr*, which is used to designate chosenness in Exodus–Deuteronomy. The new element in Genesis is the element of divine promise. Unlike the divine undertakings in the rest of the Pentateuch, which tend to be phrased 'If you do this … I will do that', the promises in Genesis are (more or less) one-sided. They indicate that Yahweh will continue to be bound by Yahweh's promises, regardless of the conduct of Abraham and his family. In some places, such as Genesis 15, the text appears to be at pains to reassure the Israelites that Yahweh will keep these promises, no matter what transpires. In Genesis 15, Abram becomes the representative of the fearful post-exilic Israelites, anxious that the promises will be broken. In Gen. 15:2 Abram responds to a promise of reward by crying 'O LORD, what will you give me, for I continue childless …' and, in 15:8, 'O LORD God, how shall I know that I am to possess it?' The rest of the chapter is full of rhetorical and literary techniques designed to persuade Abraham, and the reader, that Yahweh will keep the promises. Such reassurance was necessary after other 'everlasting' divine promises, such as the promise that the House of David would rule Israel forever (e.g. 2 Samuel 7), proved to have been broken following the return from exile.

Further elements and illustrations of the divine promises in Genesis will be discussed in Chapter 3, but one further element of Genesis' functioning as a new story of hope to the post-exilic Israelites should be noted here. The story of Mosaic Yahwism found in Exodus–Deuteronomy (and beyond) is an origins story for the nation of Israel. It tells of Yahweh's calling of a chosen people, and placement of them in their own land with their own law. Genesis widens the story. What had been a story of a nation and its God becomes a story of a God who creates Earth and the Heavens. In Genesis, Yahweh is not limited to the concept of a national god. Rather, the God of Genesis is universal – the creator (and saviour and judge) of all nations and peoples. To be sure, Israel (as represented by the Terahite family) is uniquely chosen by Yahweh in Genesis, but Yahweh is nevertheless the origin of all peoples and of Earth. In the post-exilic context this will have been significant for two reasons. First, there could be no residual questions about Yahweh's stature and power vis-à-vis other national gods. To the extent that there were other gods, they could not compete with Yahweh, who was the prime-mover of all. Second, the model of the universal creator-god had already been developing in Mesopotamia, and the exiles had been exposed to this model in Babylon. The Genesis story was, therefore, one that aspired to compete not with the stories of the nations surrounding Israel but rather with the procession of empires that sought to occupy and control it. The Yahweh of Genesis was beholden to no other god because the Yahweh of Genesis was the creator of all.

This has been a long discussion and explanation of the assertion that I made in the very first paragraph of this chapter: 'Genesis is a curated collection of stories that furnished a people in need of a future with a past.' I've argued that without a past a people cannot hope to have a future. When Genesis was written, the future of Israel was looking bleak. Genesis looked back to Israel's earliest history in order to tell a new story that could offer a new way into the future – one that avoided mere repetition of old patterns that were no longer working. This may not be the way in which you have thought about Genesis in the past, but thanks to scholarship over recent decades, it is the way in which Genesis is going to be thought about in the future.

One of the main questions raised by this scholarship is 'How, then, does Genesis relate to the story of Mosaic Yahwism that it precedes?' That will be the primary question for the next chapter, which will explore the relationships between Genesis and the books that follow it.

References

Achenbach, Reinhard. (2015), 'How to Speak about GOD with Non-Israelites: Some Observations about the Use of Names for God by Israelites and Pagans in the Pentateuch', in Frederico Giuntoli and Konrad Schmid (eds), *The Post-Priestly Pentateuch*, 35–52, FAT 101, Tübingen: Mohr Siebeck.

Brett, Mark G. (2000), *Genesis: Procreation and the Politics of Identity*, OTR, London: Routledge.

Brett, Mark G. (2018), 'YHWH among the Nations: The Politics of Divine Names in Genesis 15 and 24', in Mark G. Brett and Jakob Wöhrle (eds), *The Politics of the Ancestors*, 113–30, FAT 124, Tübingen: Mohr Siebeck.

Brett, Mark G. (2019), *Locations of God: Political Theology in the Hebrew Bible*, Oxford: Oxford University Press.

Carr, David M. (1996), *Reading the Fractures of Genesis: Historical and Literary Approaches*, Louisville, KY: Westminster John Knox Press.

Carr, David M. (2014), *Holy Resilience: The Bible's Traumatic Origins*, New Haven: Yale University Press.

De Pury, Albert. (2002), 'Gottesname, Gottesbezeichnung und Gottesbegriff: 'Elohim' als Indiz zur Entstehungsgeschichte des Pentateuch', in Jan Christian Gertz, Konrad Schmid and Markus Witte (eds), *Abschied vom Jahwisten: Die Komposition des Hexateuch in der jüngsten Diskussion*, 25–47, Berlin: Walter de Gruyter.

Frei, Peter. (2001), 'Persian Imperial Authorization: A Summary', in James W. Watts (ed.), *Persia and Torah: The Theory of Persian Imperial Authorization*, 5–40, Symposium Series 17, Atlanta, GA: SBL.

Gertz, Jan C. et al. (eds). (2016), *The Formation of the Pentateuch: Bridging the Academic Cultures of Europe, Israel and North America*, FAT 111, Tübingen: Mohr Siebeck.

Gunkel, Hermann. (1997), *Genesis*, trans. Mark E. Biddle, Macon, GA: Mercer University Press.

Habel, Norman C. (1993), *The Land Is Mine: Six Biblical Land Ideologies*, OBT, Minneapolis, MN: Fortress Press.
Hendel, Ronald. (2012), 'Historical Context', in Craig A. Evans et al. (eds), *The Book of Genesis: Composition, Reception, and Interpretation*, 51–82, VTSup 152, Atlanta, GA: SBL.
Hustvedt, Siri. (2011), *The Summer without Men*, London: Sceptre.
Knohl, Israel. (1995), *The Sanctuary of Silence: The Priestly Torah and the Holiness School*, Minneapolis, MN: Fortress Press.
Milgrom, Jacob. (2003), 'H_R in Leviticus and Elsewhere in the Torah', in Rolf Rendtorff and Robert A. Kugler (eds), *The Book of Leviticus: Composition and Reception*, 24–40, VTSup 93, Leiden: Brill.
Moberly, R.W.L. (1992), *The Old Testament of the Old Testament: Patriarchal Narratives and Mosaic Yahwism*, OBT, Minneapolis, MN: Fortress Press.
O'Connor, Kathleen M. (2018), *Genesis 1 – 25A*, Macon, GA: Smyth & Helwys.
O'Connor, Kathleen M. (2020), *Genesis 25B – 50*, Macon, GA: Smyth & Helwys.
Rendtorff, Rolf. (1990), *The Problem of the Process of Transmission in the Pentateuch*, trans. J.J. Scullion, JSOTSup 89, Sheffield: JSOT.
Römer, Thomas. (2006), 'The Elusive Yahwist: A Short History of Research', in Thomas B. Dozeman and Konrad Schmid (eds), *A Farewell to the Yahwist? The Composition of the Pentateuch in Recent European Interpretation*, 9–28, CPREI 34, Atlanta, GA: SBL.
Schmid, Konrad. (2010), *Genesis and the Moses Story: Israel's Dual Origins in the Hebrew Bible*, trans. James D. Nogalski, Siphrut 3, Winona Lake, IN: Eisenbrauns.
Schmid, Konrad. (2018), 'The Sources of the Pentateuch, Their Literary Extent and the Bridge between Genesis and Exodus: A Survey of Scholarship since Astruc', in Christoph Berner and Harald Samuel (eds), *Book Seams in the Hexateuch I*, 21–41, FAT 120, Tübingen: Mohr Siebeck.
Tobolowsky, Andrew. (2017), *The Sons of Jacob and the Sons of Herakles: The History of the Tribal System and the Organization of Tribal Identity*, Tübingen: Mohr Siebeck.
Van Seters, John. (1992), *Prologue to History: The Yahwist as Historian in Genesis*, Louisville, KY: Westminster/John Knox Press.
Warner, Megan. (2018), *Re-Imagining Abraham: A Re-Assessment of the Influence of Deuteronomism in Genesis*, OTS 72, Leiden: Brill.
Warner, Megan. (2023), *Effective Stories: Reading Genesis through the Lens of Resilience*, TB 2, Sheffield: Sheffield Phoenix Press.
Wenham, Gordon J. (1987), *Genesis 1 – 15*, WBC 2, Dallas, TX: Word Books.
Wenham, Gordon J. (1994), *Genesis 16 – 50*, WBC 2, Dallas, TX: Word Books.
Westermann, Claus. (1984), *Genesis 12 – 36*, trans. J.J. Scullion, Minneapolis: Augsburg Press.

2

Where Does Genesis Fit?

It can hardly be disputed that Genesis comes at the beginning. But the beginning of what? If it is part of the function of Genesis to act as an introduction, preface, prologue or prequel, then to what, precisely, is it the introduction, preface, prologue or prequel? And how does Genesis relate to the books that follow it? These are all ways of asking where Genesis 'fits' in the canon, and to which groupings of books Genesis belongs. This is more than a purely academic question, as the relationship between Genesis and the books following it can tell us a great deal about Genesis itself.

There has been something of a preoccupation over the last 10–20 years among scholars, and especially in Europe, with identifying and defining large literary works in the OT. By 'large literary works' I mean collections of books that appear to have shared origins or identity, or that belong together because they are of the same genre or because it is possible to identify a narrative arc, or themes and motifs, running through them. This interest has been partly prompted by the increasing complexity of historical critical approaches, particularly in pentateuchal studies. To some extent, an interest in larger literary works can be a convenient alternative focus when other avenues of enquiry seem particularly hard-going or unfruitful. On the other hand, looking at larger groupings of works can be a helpful new approach to resolving those same complexities, and new light may be shed on individual books when they are viewed in the context of their external relationships.

Scrolls and Books

A little background about books and scrolls may be helpful. The noun 'book' tends to refer to something more conceptual than it is physical when it comes to biblical literature, especially that of the OT. Today, we generally expect that a book will be a single printed volume. A physical book today usually contains a single conceptual book, unless it is an anthology. Biblical books, however, were first written on scrolls made of parchment or papyrus, and a 'scroll' and a 'book' were not necessarily the same thing. There would not have been the kind of expectation that we have today that a scroll would contain the text of a (complete) single 'book'. A scroll may have contained a single book, a portion of a book or a collection of books. The length of a literary work was a significant factor, and scroll size, too, played an important role in what was included in any given scroll. As it happens, Genesis was the right length to fit comfortably in a single scroll, although larger scrolls were capable of containing multiple books. Ancient scroll finds have varied considerably. Some contain a full copy of what we today consider to be an individual book. Some scrolls contain multiple books, such as all five books of the Pentateuch, for example. Others, including those found at Qumran, include fragments of what we today consider to be individual biblical (and extra-biblical) books. When multiple works were collected together in an individual scroll, it was not always made clear when one 'book' ended and another began, as would be the case today. The distinction was not necessarily made apparent either visually (by headings or breaks, for example) or literarily (many scholars have noted that some of the books in the Pentateuch do not have a clear beginning or introduction, but rather seem to carry on from what went before). All of this means that ancient scrolls may offer scholars clues about the origins of different books, or about original groupings of books, or even suggest that what we now think of as individual books were originally continuous compositions. On the other hand, these clues may be equivocal or even unhelpful. Identification of individual books, as well as of collections, must be made through a combination of study of ancient scrolls and of literary markers within the text.

When scholars today write about groupings of books, such as a Pentateuch, Hexateuch or Enneateuch, they may be imagining ancient scrolls that contain all of the constituent books. Alternatively, they may have a mental picture of a scroll 'library' in which scribes stored together multiple scrolls, each containing a single book, or two or three books, in a clay vessel, either for the purpose of combining the content of the scrolls into a single scroll or because that kind of storage helped to categorize groups of books for convenience or to denote relative authority. Both mental images have validity, as the physical evidence points to a range of practices. What we can't be certain about, from the physical evidence alone, is the direction in which scribes worked and what implications that might have for our understanding of the origins of biblical books and collections. Was there, for example, an initial conceptual (if not necessarily physical) larger work, such as an Enneateuch, whose contents were only later divided into individual books? If so, how large was this original work? Alternatively, were the works we now think of as books originally composed individually and only later collected together in scrolls? What we can't do, argues Thomas Römer (2011: 40–1), is conclude that a larger work was divided mechanically into smaller parts for practical reasons. He writes, 'It is immediately clear that each book of the Torah has its own profile. This is especially the case for Genesis and Deuteronomy, whereas Exodus and Leviticus are more closely connected.' Some understanding of ancient writing and scribal practices is, therefore, necessary but not decisive when it comes to assessing questions about the origins of Genesis, its membership of one or more biblical groupings, or the relationships between Genesis and the books that follow it.

Where Does Genesis Belong?

It is traditional to consider Genesis to be the first book of a five-book entity (a Pentateuch or Torah). Much of the discussion in Chapter 1 assumes this. Christians have traditionally divided the books of the OT into four sections: Pentateuch, History, Wisdom and Prophecy. The Hebrew Bible (or Tanak), conversely, has only three traditional sections: Torah, Prophets (former and latter) and Writings. Within the Jewish canon all the books between Joshua and the Books of Kings (inclusive) are categorized as prophecy. Within the Christian canon these same books are categorized as history, and often given the names 'Deuteronomistic History' or 'Primary History'. Further, within Judaism the Pentateuch enjoys a greater level of authority than the Prophets, which in turn are considered more authoritative than the Writings. Christianity has not traditionally weighted the authority of biblical books in this way.

Categorization of the OT has raised questions about the distinctiveness of the Pentateuch. If both the Pentateuchal books and the books of the Deuteronomistic History are 'history', broadly understood, and if the books of the Pentateuch have no greater stature than those of the Deuteronomistic History, are there any valid grounds for distinguishing between them? And if there are valid grounds for doing so, then where does Deuteronomy belong – with the Pentateuch or with the Deuteronomistic

History? These questions have been taken up in broader debates about the Deuteronomistic History. The term 'Deuteronomistic History' can be attributed to Martin Noth (writing in the mid-twentieth century). Prior to Noth, many scholars had been of the view that the sources of the Pentateuch, J, E and P, were not to be found only in the Pentateuch, but that they carried on into subsequent books. Noth made two arguments to support the distinctiveness of the Pentateuch, on the one hand, and the Deuteronomistic History (or Former Prophets), on the other. First, he argued that Joshua must be interpreted without recourse to the Newer Documentary Hypothesis, and that J, E and P were not to be found in Joshua. Second, Noth maintained that no sign of Deuteronomistic editing was to be found anywhere in Genesis, Exodus, Leviticus or Numbers. Noth's arguments suggested that the Pentateuch and Deuteronomistic History were fundamentally different, and the separation between the two in Christian scholarship can be attributed to his work.

Konrad Schmid argues that Noth's arguments were successful, and his Deuteronomistic History hypothesis persuasive, because of an ironic compromise reached between Noth and Gerhard von Rad. At roughly the same time as Noth was publishing his commentary on Joshua, in which these arguments were made, von Rad was publishing his own arguments about the existence of a six-book 'Hexateuch', in which a narrative arc extended from Genesis through to Joshua. Von Rad's work was inherently at odds with that of Noth. Schmid writes that both Noth and von Rad made compromises. Von Rad hypothesized that an earlier form of Joshua had included material from J, E and P, but that this material had been omitted when the Hexateuch had been combined with the Deuteronomistic History. Noth, for his part, accepted von Rad's hypothesis that a Hexateuch had preceded the Pentateuch (from which Joshua had been excised), despite the fact that, as Schmid argues (2011: 17), this acceptance was 'rather surprising since Noth had developed a completely different approach to the composition of the Pentateuch'.

Following the challenges to source-critical theory of the 1970s, outlined in Chapter 1, the question of the separation between the Pentateuch and Deuteronomistic History once again became live, at least in Europe. The model for the composition of the Pentateuch put forward by Rendtorff was remarkably similar to Noth's own model for the composition of the Deuteronomistic History, so that the two groups of books could be seen to be closer to one another than Noth himself had allowed. Rendtorff's work was further developed by Erhard Blum, who argued that the Pentateuch was essentially a composite document of P and D materials. This is the approach now taken by most English-language introductions to the OT. Importantly for our purposes, Blum revisited and revised his argument in 2002. He drew a distinction between Genesis and the books that follow it, suggesting that the mix of P and D documents that characterizes Exodus to II Kings is not characteristic of Genesis. As Schmid (2011: 22) observes, 'It is quite obvious that the "Deuteronomistic" idiom can be found more clearly in Exodus and Numbers than in Genesis.' If the erstwhile pentateuchal books were now best understood as elements of an extended Deuteronomistic History, then the impact of Blum's re-assessment was that there must be seen to be a very real question mark about the place of Genesis in that Deuteronomistic History. Around the same time, de Pury, Römer and Schmid were arguing that the literary linking of Genesis with Exodus had occurred relatively late and, in any event, did not predate P. This argument is outlined in Chapter 1 of this book. As a result of both developments, the acknowledgement of a distinctive lack of D presence in Genesis, and recognition of the lack of an early literary connection between Genesis and Exodus, the place of Genesis in larger book complexes was put in doubt.

These were not the only responses to what Schmid argues was the end of the separation between the Pentateuch and the Deuteronomistic History. One was the adoption of alternative names for the longer complex, Genesis to II Kings, that avoided the connotations of the 'Deuteronomistic' tag. One of these alternatives was the title 'Primary History', which had already been proposed by David Noel Freedman in 1962. Another was 'Enneateuch', a name that did no more than identify a collection of eleven books. ('Enneateuch' is usually taken to mean a grouping of the first seven books, plus the books of Samuel and Kings, and not including Ruth, that can be counted either as nine or eleven books, depending on how one counts the volumes of Samuel and Kings.) Of those who continued to favour 'Deuteronomistic History', some proposed speaking of 'Deuteronomistic Histories', some of which might include Genesis, while others might not. Another proposal took into account the manifest similarities and links between Genesis and Leviticus, neither of which showed much evidence of participation, or interest, in a 'Deuteronomistic History'. As part of this proposal, an essentially Priestly 'Triteuch' of three books – Genesis, Exodus and Leviticus – was hypothesized. Although ostensibly Priestly, Numbers was excluded from this grouping, largely because its late dating and distinctive themes were thought to have set it apart from the particular brand of Priestly thought in evidence in Genesis and Leviticus.

Where does this weighty history of scholarship leave Genesis? Where, in the wake of these discussions, might Genesis be said to 'fit'? A plethora of potential perspectives suggest themselves, each with its own implications for interpretation of Genesis as a book:

1. Genesis is the first book of a five-book Pentateuch. It opens a narrative arc that is resolved, and introduces themes and motifs that are continued, in Deuteronomy, the book that closes the grouping;
2. before Genesis belonged to a Pentateuch, it was the first book of a six-book Hexateuch. It opens a narrative arc that is resolved, and introduces themes and motifs that are continued, in Joshua, the book that closes the grouping;
3. Genesis is the first book of a four-book Tetrateuch. It opens a narrative arc that is resolved, and introduces themes and motifs that are continued, in Numbers, the book that closes the grouping. The next grouping, the Deuteronomistic History, begins with Deuteronomy;
4. Genesis is the first book of a three-book Triteuch. It opens a narrative arc that is resolved, and introduces themes and motifs that are continued, in Leviticus, the book that closes the grouping;
5. Genesis is the first book of an eleven-book Enneateuch (or some form of 'Deuteronomistic History'). It opens a narrative arc that is resolved, and introduces themes and motifs that are continued, in II Kings, the book that closes the grouping; or
6. Genesis is sufficiently different from the books that follow it that it should not be considered to belong to any of the above groupings. It is at once introductory and self-contained. Some elements of its narrative arc are resolved within its own pages, while some are introductory. Some of its themes and motifs are distinctive or unique, while others appear to have been added for the purpose of building links with other book complexes. To the extent that Genesis is 'introductory', it could be considered introductory to the Old Testament as a whole, or even to both Christian testaments, just as readily as it can be considered introductory to smaller groups of books, such as a Pentateuch or Hexateuch.

The remainder of this chapter draws out and explores the particular implications for interpretation of Genesis that arise from each of these potential perspectives.

Genesis as the First Book of the Pentateuch

Approaching Genesis as the first book of the Pentateuch has the effect of drawing our attention to those particular themes and motifs within Genesis that are common to all five Pentateuchal books. These themes and motifs include, most particularly, the blessings and promises to the ancestors, Abraham and his descendants, which demonstrate an apparent correspondence with related material found throughout the five books, but particularly in Deuteronomy. Foremost among these is a tradition of a promise, formulated as an oath made to Abraham and extended subsequently to Isaac and Jacob, to give the land to them. Although there are references throughout Genesis to a divine land promise, the verses most closely associated with the 'land-promise-as-oath' tradition are Gen. 22:15-18 (Abraham), 26:3-5 (Isaac) and 50:24. The first two of these passages are closely connected, and together record the circumstances in which the oath promise was made, albeit somewhat obliquely. Deuteronomy contains many verses referring to a promise, made by oath, to give the land to ancestors. There is a catch, however. Two scholars, Van Seters (1975) and Römer (1990) (one North American and one European), have shown that most of these verses do not refer to the ancestors of Genesis but rather to the first exodus generation. Although some of the Deuteronomy verses do refer to Abraham, Isaac and Jacob by name, Van Seters and Römer argue that the names were added in a later revision of the text that was part of a project to draw Genesis and Deuteronomy together under the pentateuchal umbrella. These arguments of Van Seters and Römer have largely been accepted (although, as I will explain in the next section, some see here not a pentateuchal but a hexateuchal project). Schmid (2010) has argued that there is at least one verse related to the land-promise-as-oath tradition found in each book of the Pentateuch: Gen. 50:24; Exod. 23:13 and 33:1; Num. 32:11 and Deut. 34:4. He also tentatively includes Lev. 26:42 as a member of this group, even though it doesn't contain an oath reference. All of these verses, Schmid argues further, post-date the Priestly material in Genesis.

The implication of these arguments is that, while common themes and motifs can be identified in Genesis and Deuteronomy, and while a narrative arc can be identified, in which promises made in Genesis are on the verge of being fulfilled in Deuteronomy, the relevant parts of the text appear to have been added as part of a project to construct a Pentateuch, rather than having been original to either Genesis or the other pentateuchal books, including Deuteronomy. Other links between Genesis and Deuteronomy have also been identified but these, too, have generally been explained as later, redactional additions, designed either to connect Genesis with Exodus or to build a Pentateuch. For example, the brief conclusion to Deuteronomy in Deuteronomy 34 contains several references back to Genesis, some explicit, such as the naming of Abraham, Isaac and Jacob in connection with the oath-based divine land promise (Deut. 34:4), and some implicit, such as the age of Moses at the time of his death (Deut. 34:7), which alludes to Yahweh's pronouncement in Gen. 6:3 that henceforth the maximum age of humans would be 120 years.

These redactional additions to Genesis, which appear to have been added for the purposes of building links between Genesis and Deuteronomy, have often been considered to be Deuteronomistic or semi-Deuteronomistic in nature. As indicated already, the question whether Genesis contains any traces of D has been keenly debated. Both Noth and Blum (in his 2002 revisions) have denied the presence of D in Genesis. Nevertheless, other scholars have, over time, written about what they see as D-influenced additions to Genesis, which have included the passages already referred to, with the addition of Genesis 15 and Gen. 18:17-19, in particular. This is part of a broader development in scholarship, connected with the trend of characterizing post-exilic literature (especially, though not limited to, pentateuchal literature) as either broadly Priestly or Deuteronomistic. Rendtorff, Carr, Ausloos and others have cautioned against an over-readiness to characterize literature as Deuteronomistic, a tendency termed, in a 1999 collection of essays, titled *Those Elusive Deuteronomists*, 'pan-Deuteronomism'. One of the problems associated with attaching the label 'D' or 'semi-D' to text is that it encourages readers to interpret that text in line with theology or ideology associated with D. This can have a very significant impact upon assessments of the meaning and outlook of that text. In *Re-Imagining Abraham: A Re-Assessment of the Influence of Deuteronomism in Genesis* (Warner 2018), I argued that, although some redactional material in Genesis, and particularly the passages already mentioned here, uses (semi-)Deuteronomistic language, themes and motifs, close and contextual reading of that material does not indicate an intent to import into Genesis Deuteronomic theology or ideology. On the contrary, it indicates an intention to resist or even subvert that theology or ideology. I identified a consistent pattern of use of (quasi) Deuteronomistic language, themes and motifs in ways that differed markedly from the ways in which the same language, themes and motifs are used in Deuteronomy. As a consequence, I argued, material in Genesis that was universalist or inclusive in character had consistently and wrongly been interpreted as particular or exclusivist, with important implications for our understanding of the meaning of Genesis.

Genesis as the First Book of the Hexateuch

Many scholars now agree that a redaction project designed to shape a Hexateuch preceded the Pentateuch redaction. What those scholars envisage is that scribes added text, notably to Genesis and Joshua, to create a recognizable six-book entity. Subsequently, other scribes added yet more text (including the passages discussed above) in order to create a Pentateuch that excised Joshua and its conquest account, shunting it into the Deuteronomistic History.

The strongest evidence for a hexateuchal redaction is the existence of Joshua 24. This chapter differs in style and content from Joshua 23, and it contains a comprehensive summary of Israelite history, including the history of the ancestors, that serves to draw that period of history together and to bring it to an end. The strongest link with Joshua 24 in Genesis is found in the non-P Abram covenant account in Genesis 15. Numerous scholars, including Carr, have pointed to parallels between Genesis 15 and Joshua 24 in support of their argument that Genesis 15 (possibly in its entirety) was added to Genesis as part of a project to create a Hexateuch. The same scholars have also argued that Abram's dream (or vision?) described in Gen. 15:13-15 is a prediction of the exodus, designed to build links with the Book of Exodus, and that the initial building of links between Genesis and Exodus was an element of a hexateuchal, rather than pentateuchal, project.

The distinction between a Hexateuch and a Pentateuch is not insignificant. The narrative arcs of the two conceptualized book complexes are quite different. A Hexateuch tells a story of promise made and fulfilled, with a particular focus on a land promise. The fulfillment of the land promise is achieved, in this story arc, through violent, divinely sponsored, military encounter. Further, the understanding of the land promise itself is exclusivist, in that it assumes that the Israelites must be allowed exclusive possession of Canaan and that the promise entails a responsibility to remove other peoples from the land. One can imagine how, in the wake of the Babylonian defeat and exile, this story might have lost its lustre. The Israelites had been given the land via military success and had lost it again through military defeat. The golden age of Israel had come and gone. The pentateuchal story, on the other hand, is different. In a Pentateuch that ends with the people in Moab, on the verge of entering the land, the promises are still extant. The golden age is yet to come. The role of Genesis is particularly significant in a Pentateuch, because Genesis is a book of promises – promises that pre-date the Torah and that had not been spoiled by Israel's Torah failures. Further, the Priestly character of Genesis is significant. Abraham, in particular, is depicted as living in a far more inclusivist manner than that advocated by Deuteronomy. Genesis (as redacted) portrays Abraham as an outsider who comes to live in Canaan, relatively peacefully, alongside the other peoples already living there. The Priestly conception of the possession of land (and therefore of the land promise), which is far less exclusivist than that of D (see the discussion in Chapter 3), is reflected in the depiction of the lives of Abraham and his families, lived among other peoples in the land.

Even if the theme of promise, and, in particular, of a divine land promise, is central to both the Hexateuch and the Pentateuch, Genesis takes on a different kind of significance in the two groupings of books. The Hexateuch and Pentateuch hark back to different elements in Genesis. One thing that they both do, however, is to remind the interpreter that the promise material in Genesis is not original to it. There was a time when the divine promises to Abraham and his descendants were not a part of Genesis, so that the meaning of Genesis had to be found elsewhere. Genesis (or its constituent parts) was perhaps once a collection of stories told for their own sake, and not for the sake of offering traumatized Israelites a way forward into the future.

Genesis as the First Book of the Tetrateuch

The idea of a Tetrateuch (i.e. a four-book collection comprising Genesis, Exodus, Leviticus and Numbers) is less familiar than the idea of either a Pentateuch or a Hexateuch. Nor do we have evidence that scribes ever intentionally set about creating a Tetrateuch in the same way that we have evidence of pentateuchal and hexateuchal redactions. The idea of a Tetrateuch is mostly about what the Torah looks like if Deuteronomy is conceptualized as belonging not to it but to the Deuteronomistic History. The difference is perhaps greater than it sounds. The influence of Deuteronomy upon the interpretation of the rest of the Torah has been significant. It appears that, in the period of the return from the exile, Deuteronomy functioned as a kind of constitution in Judah. The Torah might have reflected a compromise between the theologies of P and D, but it seems from the biblical evidence that D was, in the post-return period, a 'majority' position, while P's was, in many senses, an 'alternative' or 'minority' outlook. The books of Ezra and Nehemiah, which recount some of the history of the period, tend to support this idea. Certainly, most of Ezra's programmes, and the 'Torah' to which he claimed to be returning, indicate the strong influence of Deuteronomy and Deuteronomistic ideas. The concept of a Tetrateuch, from which Deuteronomy is absent, allows the reader to bring Genesis, along with Exodus–Numbers, out of the shadows of Deuteronomy, and to read it on its own terms, which includes allowing more space for its Priestly elements.

Genesis as the First Book of the Triteuch

The idea of a Priestly Triteuch (sometimes written 'Triateuch' – a three-book collection including Genesis, Exodus and Leviticus) is more recent than the ideas of any of the book complexes already discussed. Those whose work has been influential in the development of the concept of a Triteuch include Thomas Römer, Reinhard Achenbach, Christophe Nihan and Rainer Albertz. Although each of these scholars is European, their thinking builds on the work of Israeli scholar Israel Knohl, who influentially developed a theory of a Holiness School responsible for Leviticus 17–26 (1994).

Central to the concept of a Triteuch is the idea that the conclusion to Leviticus found in Chapters 17–26 also functions as a conclusion to the Priestly material in Genesis and Exodus. Crucially, for our purposes, an element of this idea is a conviction that these chapters of Leviticus, which can conveniently be termed 'holiness legislation', or H, look back to the creation narratives of Genesis, and aspire to a return to Yahweh's world as it is portrayed prior to the flood (Genesis 6–9), in which Yahweh dwelt among humans on Earth. In particular, as Brett (2019) has argued, the holiness legislation picks up on Genesis' distinctive depiction of the earliest humans 'walking with God'. In Lev. 26:12 Yahweh promise to 'walk about with' the Israelites if they keep Yahweh's Torah. The unusual, reflexive, Hebrew form (or 'stem') of the verb 'to walk' in Lev. 26:12 harks back to the use of the same stem in Gen. 3:8, in which Adam and Eve hear the sound of Yahweh Elohim 'walking about' in the garden. Further, although prior to the flood humans 'walked with' Elohim (Enoch in Gen. 5:22, 24 and Noah in 6:9), following the flood there is no further instance of this motif. After the flood, humans walk 'before' Yahweh (most notably kings – see the further discussion below), 'in the way of' Yahweh, or 'in Yahweh's statutes'. The centrality of holiness within the ideology of Leviticus 17–26 reflects the aspiration to return to a time when Yahweh walked among humans. The holiness legislation is concerned with creating holy space, fit for Yahweh's habitation, and where Yahweh can 'walk about' with humans. Further, the holiness legislation seeks to extend the sphere of this holy space outwards from the temple (or tabernacle) to the whole camp, and eventually throughout the land. For H, Yahweh's creation is not automatically holy but it can be made so through observance of the Torah. If people keep Yahweh's Torah, so that the whole land (or even 'lands', cf. Gen. 26:3-4) is holy, then Yahweh can dwell in any part of it, with Yahweh's people. The sting of exile is removed if the Israelites can be 'with' Yahweh regardless of where, geographically, they find themselves.

For Genesis, the implications of being the first of a three-book Triteuch are considerable. A framework comprising Genesis 1–3 and Leviticus 26 has the effect that Genesis' account of creation, and particularly the story of the garden, becomes not merely an account of the distant past but an aspirational model for Israel's future.

There is a technical issue here that deserves noting. The Garden of Eden story, in Genesis 2–3, is traditionally classified as non-P. How then can it be argued that this text comprises part of a Priestly frame with Leviticus 26? Brett (2019) tackles this problem head-on. Building on Blum's earlier conception of P and D 'compositions', in which earlier texts are collected and included by P and D along with their own material, Brett argues that the Eden story can be conceptualized as a story adopted and used by P, for its own purposes, even though P has its own creation account in Gen. 1–2:4a. He writes (2019: 67), 'In short, the Priestly composition has embraced the Eden narrative and imagines the restoration of Eden within the cult and its associated land.'

The creation narratives are not the only aspect of Genesis to which Leviticus 26 harks back. Lev. 26:40-45 introduces an extremely significant element of H's theology, and Genesis' ancestral traditions play a central role within it. I referred above to the conditionality of the covenant promise in Leviticus 26 – Yahweh would walk with the Israelites *if* they kept the Torah. The holiness legislation incorporates the conditionality of D in this regard. However, Leviticus 26 introduces an innovation over Deuteronomy 28 (D's equivalent catalogue of the blessings that would follow from obedience and the curses that would follow from disobedience). Lev. 26:40-45 announces the possibility of divine forgiveness for Israelites who confess their wrongdoing (and that of their forebears), humble their hearts and make amends. When Israelites repent in this way, the passage says, Yahweh will remember the covenant with Jacob, Isaac and Abraham (this is the only place in the OT in which the ancestral triad is inverted) and will remember the land, and so not destroy them utterly. The idea of the association of Yahweh's *remembrance* of individuals with Yahweh's acts of salvation is evidenced throughout the Triteuch in Priestly (and post-Priestly) texts. In Gen. 8:1 Elohim *remembers* Noah and the animals with him in the ark and causes the flood waters to subside. In Gen. 30:22 Elohim *remembers* Rachel and grants her a child. In Gen. 19:29, Elohim *remembers* Abraham and saves Lot on Abraham's account. The idea of the ancestors as 'memory objects' is developed even further in an added passage in the Golden Calf story in Exod. 32:13, in which Moses implores Yahweh to *remember* Yahweh's servants, Abraham, Isaac and Jacob, and the oath Yahweh swore to them, and thus to save the Israelites. Exod. 32:13 is carefully phrased to allude back to Gen. 22:15-18 and 26:3-5, and thus can be seen to be part of a project to bind Genesis, Exodus and Leviticus together.

As the first book of a Priestly Triteuch, then, Genesis plays a central role in setting up the foundations of Priestly theology. This is not necessarily to suggest that scribes set out, explicitly, to create a three-book entity, or that the three books were ever incorporated in a single scroll. An alternative way of understanding the Triteuch is to see it as the heart of a Priestly Pentateuch, in which Leviticus is not the final but the *central* book (perhaps in a parallel to the idea of the location of the sanctuary at the centre of the Temple precinct). Either way, Genesis sets up themes, motifs and stories that become central to the theology of the larger, Priestly, complex.

Genesis as the First Book of the Enneateuch

Scholars are divided about whether an eleven-book Enneateuch pre- or post-dates the creation of the Hexateuch and Pentateuch. Was there an epic initial history of Israel, before divisions into Hexateuch and the Pentateuch occurred? Or alternatively, was an Enneatuech 'formed' by the combination of Pentateuch and Deuteronomistic History, perhaps with Joshua as a literary 'hinge'? A literary eleven-book 'work' has been recognized since at least the seventeenth century, but the question of how and when it arose continues to divide scholarly opinion. Joseph Blenkinsopp (1992: 34) has characterized Genesis 1 through to 2 Kings 25 as a national epic that presents 'a continuous history from creation to exile'. The problem of the connection between Genesis and Exodus, or, rather, the lack of such a connection prior to P, as already discussed, increasingly causes problems for scholars. There cannot be, they argue, an eleven-book pre-P history of Israel if the ancestral and Mosaic traditions were not joined prior to P. As a result, some scholars posit an Enneateuch that does not contain Genesis (so not really an 'Enneateuch' at all!) Some, too, question whether Deuteronomy was initially part of an extended collection, such as an Enneateuch, or whether it existed, until relatively late, as an independent book. For further discussion of these issues see Dozeman, Römer and Schmid's book *Pentateuch, Hexateuch or Enneateuch?*

Both the existence of an entity properly identifiable as 'Enneateuch' and the place of Genesis in it are, therefore, open to debate. My own work has, however, suggested to me that authors of various texts in Genesis, across multiple schools or affiliations, understood themselves to be writing with an enneateuchal horizon. One of the less-recognized characteristics of Genesis is its propensity for engaging with themes of monarchy. Of course, there is no Israelite king in Genesis – that is a development from much later in the enneateuchal story. However, if Genesis was being written, as much of it was, in a time when the monarchy had been lost (i.e. in the years following the return from exile), then Genesis is a story or stories from a time when the question 'if not monarchy, then what?' was live. Even though Genesis does not portray an Israelite kingship, its pages acknowledge the kings of other nations (with whom the ancestors engaged from time to time), and monarchic language and themes, both explicit and implicit, can be found across its various sections. In Genesis 1, for example, Elohim creates human beings to have 'dominion' over fish, birds and animals, and exhorts them to do precisely that. The language of 'subduing' the earth also has monarchic overtones. The Joseph Story, too, opens with monarchic language. In Genesis 37 Joseph dreams that his family bows down to him. His brothers, resenting the implications of these dreams, ask, 'Are you indeed to reign over us? Are you indeed to have dominion over us?' (Gen. 37:8). Numerous scholars have observed a raft of parallels between the character of Joseph and that of David, proposing that Joseph might be considered a 'prolepsis' of David (i.e. a character who anticipates David – a kind of reverse echo). Elsewhere, I have argued that something of a royal battle is waged through the pages of the Joseph Story between Joseph and his brother Judah, eventually won by Judah (Warner 2023). Judah's victory can be perceived most clearly in the fact that in the blessings pronounced over his sons by Jacob in Genesis 49 (at least in the Masoretic Text), the royal language is reserved for Judah: 'The sceptre shall not pass from Judah, nor the ruler's staff from between his feet, until tribute comes to him; and the obedience of the peoples is his' (Gen. 49:10). (I have specified the Masoretic Text because in the Septuagint the text is markedly different and the idea of Joseph as leader appears to be preserved.)

It is perhaps in the Abraham Cycle, however, that monarchic language and themes are most prominent. Parallels between Abraham and David, too, have often been observed. Some monarchic language is explicit – some less so. Examples of both can be found in Genesis 17. In vv. 6 and 16 Elohim tells Abraham that kings shall come from him and from Sarah (whose new name in v. 15 means 'princess'), while Ishmael will be the father of twelve princes. These examples are very clear, but readers may miss the royal allusion in Gen. 17:1: 'walk before me and be blameless (*tammim*)'. 'Walking before' Yahweh was something that Israelite kings were called to do – in fact, it might be said that 'walking before' Yahweh was a summary of all that a king was called to do. In 1 Kings 9, for example, Yahweh tells Solomon that if he walks before Yahweh, as his father David had done, with integrity (*tammim*) of heart, keeping the Torah, Yahweh would establish his throne for eternity.

Extensive parallels between the story of Abraham's life and that of David, moreover, have been noted by many scholars, including John Van Seters, Ronald Clements and Graeme Auld. My work has led me to believe that these parallels are not merely extensive but structural – in other words, that the Abraham Cycle is structured to represent the story of David in a context in which the monarchy is no more. Abraham is presented both as king and 'not king'. The result, I have argued (Warner 2017, 2018), is a narrative democratization of the monarchy, centred on Abraham and his family. In Gen. 18:19, for example, Abraham is made responsible for the teaching, by each generation of his family of the next, of 'righteousness and justice' (the syntax of Gen. 18:19 is torturous, rather like the syntax of *this* sentence). 'Righteousness and justice' is an inversion of the monarch's core responsibility, to do 'justice and righteousness'. See, for example, 2 Sam 8:15: 'So David reigned over all Israel, and David administered justice and righteousness to all his people'. (There is no other reference to justice and righteousness in the Torah, or indeed anywhere else prior to 2 Sam 8:15.) In this way, the core responsibility of the king is shared out among the members of Abraham's family and his 'house' (*beyt*) (Gen. 18:19).

One of the main themes of Genesis, the identification of the chosen son in each new generation, is highly reminiscent of monarchic narratives. There has been some scholarly dispute about whether Yahweh makes a new covenant with each new generation of Abraham's family in Genesis. In my view the better reading is that the covenant is made only once, with Abraham (albeit in two accounts, Genesis 15 and 17), and the promises and blessings passed down to his sons, just as the crown is passed down from father to son in the monarchic context. The clearest example of this process is found in Gen. 26:3-5, 24, where the covenant promises and blessings are passed on to Isaac immediately following Abraham's death. Gen. 26:5 uses a frankly remarkable amount of language to this end that is found in classic passages from Kings concerning the succession from David to Solomon, and especially in 2 Kings 2 and 9. The language is 'remarkable' because it is explicitly 'Torah' language, which the editors of Genesis are otherwise at pains to avoid. This is the explanation for Gen. 26:5's anomalous claim that Abraham was observant of Torah (before it had been handed down).

I've already argued that one of the purposes of Genesis' borrowing of royal language and themes is to portray (or effect) a democratization of royal function for a society without a monarchy. There is one further purpose, and it relates to the conditionality of the divine promise of an everlasting monarchy, especially as portrayed in 2 Kings. I will state this purpose as briefly as possible. Interested readers can see more in my *Re-Imagining Abraham* (2018). I have referred a number of times already to Gen. 22:15-18 and 26:5. The combined effect of these verses is to make YHWH's promise to Abraham either unconditional or (better, in my view) *conditional upon an already performed condition* – Abraham's obedience to the divine voice at Moriah (Genesis 22). In Genesis 26 Yahweh tells Isaac that the promise will be extended to him *because* Abraham kept the Torah. The parallels between Gen. 26:3-5 and 22:15-18 are such that scholars have accepted that it is Abraham's actions at Moriah that must be in view in Genesis 26. Moberly (1988), for example, has argued that, in the light of Genesis 26, the divine promise will henceforth be guaranteed both by Yahweh's faithfulness and Abraham's actions at Moriah. In other words, no failure of Torah observance on Isaac's part will void the promises – they are guaranteed by what Abraham has already done.

I noted above that a third verse is closely associated with Gen. 22:15-18 and 26:3-5. That verse is Exod. 32:13, which can be found in the Exodus account of the Golden Calf crisis. The Golden Calf story is itself an account built upon narrative from Kings. It functions to bring forward into the wilderness experience the 'greatest disobedience' of the OT, Jeroboam's building of a Golden Calf in 1 Kings 12. It also functions to illustrate a different outcome. In 1 Kings, the outcome of Jeroboam's sin is the exile of the Northern Kingdom to Assyria. In Exodus 32, Yahweh threatens to destroy the people; however, the punishment is stayed after Moses intercedes on the people's behalf, exhorting Yahweh to 'remember Abraham, Isaac and Jacob, your servants …'. Moses' intercession is effective, indicating that the merit of Abraham (and his family) is sufficient to counter *even the greatest* failure of Torah faithfulness.

These monarchic parallels and references indicate that part of the project of Genesis (as redacted) is to build a new foundation for Israel's trust in Yahweh's promises, after that trust had been destroyed following the failure of the divine promises that there would always be a descendant of David on the throne of Israel. Genesis does not engage only with the pentateuchal story. It is intimately concerned with the fate of Israel following the disaster of the Babylonian defeat, and particularly with the impact of that defeat upon the monarchy. Genesis is a place where Israelite scribes map out a new future for Israel in a time without a monarchy. Reading Genesis as the first book of an Enneateuch – however that Enneateuch is conceptualized – helps to bring out this aspect of Genesis' concerns and functions.

Genesis as Independent

A final approach is slightly hypothetical, in that scholars have been able to point to compelling evidence that Genesis belongs to a range of book groupings, as already outlined above. Nevertheless, this sixth approach facilitates two principal observations:

1 there is insufficiently compelling evidence to establish Genesis' membership of any one of these groupings of biblical books to the exclusion of others; and
2 clear discontinuities between Genesis and Exodus (which are not matched by discontinuities between other Pentateuchal books, such as Exodus and Leviticus, for example) witness to a degree of independence for Genesis.

I have referred already to recent work that points to the distinctiveness of Genesis and, in particular, to the lack of a literary link between Genesis and Exodus that predates P. This argument can be disorienting when first encountered, as its implications are wide-reaching. As Schmid has argued, it is possible, or even likely, that the exiles, while in exile, did not know of a history in which an ancestral period preceded an exodus from Egypt. Rather, if both traditions were well-known, they are likely to have been known as existing side by side as alternatives. Schmid has written extensively about the differences between Genesis and Exodus, although these differences have long been noticed, and I referred in Chapter 1 to Moberly's description of Genesis as 'The Old Testament of the Old Testament' (1991). The differences go far beyond an observation of the lack of a genuine literary link between the two books. It would be difficult to improve upon Schmid's own statement of the differences (2012: 188) that summarizes his more extensive discussion in *Genesis and the Moses Story*:

> Furthermore, in terms of their concerns, their theological shape, and their wording, Genesis and Exodus are indeed quite different. Genesis offers a family story; Exodus presents a story of a people. Genesis is mainly autochthonous [i.e. a story of people who are native to the land] and inclusive, while Exodus is allochthonous [i.e. a story of people who have entered the land from elsewhere] and exclusive. In the patriarchal narratives Genesis constructs a picture of the origin of Israel in its own land, and the story is both politically and theologically inclusive. The gods of Canaan can be identified with YHWH, as can be deduced from the religious-historical background of cult legends like Gen 28,11-19 or Gen 32,23-33, and the patriarchs dwell together with the inhabitants of the land and make treaties with them. Exodus, on the other hand, stresses Israel's origin abroad in Egypt and puts forward an exclusively theological argument; YHWH is a jealous

God who does not tolerate any other gods besides himself (Exod. 20,3-5; 34,14), and the Israelites shall not make peace with the inhabitants of the land (cf. Exod. 32,23-33; 34,12.15; Deut. 12,29-31; 16,21; 20,16-17; 25,19). The theological substance of Genesis and Exodus is so divergent that it is unconvincing to conclude that there is no break whatsoever between these books. [Material in square brackets is not original to Schmid, but added for the purpose of clarification.]

These differences, outlined by Schmid, are so fundamental, and so marked, that one is justified in asking to what extent Genesis could properly be considered to function in an 'introductory' sense to any grouping of books of which Exodus is a member. My own response to this has been to label Genesis a 'prequel' to Exodus (and the story of Mosaic Yahwism more generally) (Warner 2017). The genre 'prequel' differs from those such as 'introduction', 'preface' or 'prologue' in that it is inherently subversive. A prequel, by its nature, changes a reader's (or viewer's) perception of the principal work that it precedes. A perceptive reader's view of Exodus (and the books that follow it) must differ markedly, depending on whether or not she has first encountered Genesis.

The next chapter offers an exploration of the principal themes and theology of Genesis that puts some flesh upon the bones of Schmid's summary, reproduced above.

References

Auld, Graeme. (2011), 'Reading Genesis after Samuel', in Thomas B. Dozeman, Konrad Schmid and Baruch J. Schwartz (eds), *The Pentateuch: International Perspectives on Current Research*, 459–71, FAT 78, Tübingen: Mohr Siebeck.

Ausloos, Hans. (2015), *The Deuteronomist's History: The Role of the Deuteronomist in Historical-Critical Research into Genesis-Numbers*, OTS 67, Leiden: Brill.

Blenkinsopp, Joseph. (1992), *The Pentateuch: An Introduction to the First Five Books of the Bible*, New York: Doubleday.

Blum, Erhard. (2002), 'Die literarische Verbindung von Erzvätern und Exodus: Ein Gespräch mit neueren Endredaktionshypothesen', in Jan Christian Gertz, Konrad Schmid and Markus Witte (eds), *Abschied vom Jahwisten: Die Komposition des Hexateuch in der jüngsten Diskussion*, 119–56, Berlin: Walter de Gruyter.

Brett, Mark G. (2019), *Locations of God: Political Theology in the Hebrew Bible*, Oxford: Oxford University Press.

Carr, David M. (2006), 'What Is Required to Identify Pre-Priestly Narrative Connections between Genesis and Exodus? Some General reflections and Specific Cases', in Thomas B. Dozeman and Konrad Schmid (eds), *A Farewell to the Yahwist? The Composition of the Pentateuch in Recent European Interpretation*, 159–80, CPREI 34, Atlanta, GA: SBL.

Clements, Ronald. (1967), *Abraham and David: Genesis 15 and Its Meaning for Israelite Tradition*, SBT 12, London: SCM.

Dozeman, Thomas B., Thomas Römer and Konrad Schmid (eds). (2011), *Pentateuch, Hexateuch or Enneateuch: Identifying Literary Works in Genesis through Kings*, AIL 8, Atlanta, GA: SBL.

Freedman, David Noel. (1993), *The Unity of the Hebrew Bible*, Ann Arbor, MN: Michigan University Press.

Knohl, Israel. (1994), *The Sanctuary of Silence: The Priestly Torah and the Holiness School*, Minneapolis, MN: Fortress Press.

Moberly, R.W.L. (1988), 'The Earliest Commentary on the Akedah', *VT* 38: 302–23.

Moberly, R.W.L. (1992), *The Old Testament of the Old Testament: Patriarchal Narratives and Mosaic Yahwism*, OBT, Minneapolis, MN: Fortress Press.

Rendtorff, Rolf. (1990), *The Problem of the Process of Transmission in the Pentateuch*, trans. J.J. Scullion, JSOTSup 89, Sheffield: JSOT.

Römer, Thomas. (1990), *Israels Väter: Untersuschungen zu Vaterthematik im Deuteronomium und in der deuteronomistischen Tradition*, OBO 99, Göttingen: Vandenhoeck & Ruprecht.

Römer, Thomas. (2011), 'How Many Books (teuchs): Pentateuch, Hexateuch, Deuteronomistic History or Enneateuch?', in Thomas B. Dozeman, Thomas Römer and Konrad Schmid (eds), *Pentateuch, Hexateuch or Enneateuch: Identifying Literary Works in Genesis through Kings*, 25–42, AIL 8, Atlanta, GA: SBL.

Schmid, Konrad. (2010), *Genesis and the Moses Story: Israel's Dual Origins in the Hebrew Bible*, trans. James D. Nogalski, Siphrut 3, Winona Lake, IN: Eisenbrauns.

Schmid, Konrad. (2011), 'The Emergence and Separation of the Pentateuch and Deuteronomistic History in Biblical Studies', in Thomas B. Dozeman, Thomas Römer and Konrad Schmid (eds), *Pentateuch, Hexateuch or Enneateuch: Identifying Literary Works in Genesis through Kings*, 11–24, AIL 8, Atlanta, GA: SBL.

Schmid, Konrad. (2012), 'Genesis in the Pentateuch', in Craig A. Evans et al. (eds), *The Book of Genesis: Composition, Reception and Interpretation*, 27–50, VTSup 152, Atlanta, GA: SBL.

Shearing, Linda S. and Stephen L. McKenzie (eds). (1999), *Those Elusive Deuteronomists: The Phenomenon of Pan-Deuteronomism*, Sheffield: Sheffield Academic Press.

Van Seters, John. (1975), *Abraham in History and Tradition*, New Haven, CN: Yale University Press.

Van Seters, John. (1992), *Prologue to History: The Yahwist as Historian in Genesis*, Louisville, KY: Westminster/John Knox Press.

Warner, Megan. (2017), 'Back to the Future: Abraham the Prequel?', *BibInt* 25: 479–96.

Warner, Megan. (2018), *Re-Imagining Abraham: A Re-assessment of the Influence of Deuteronomism in Genesis*, OTS 72, Leiden: Brill.

Warner, Megan. (2023), '"Are You Indeed to Reign over Us?": The Politics of Genesis 37 – 50', in Mark G. Brett and Rachelle Gilmour (eds.), *Political Theologies in the Hebrew Bible*, 193–206, JAJ Sup, Leiden: Brill.

3

Themes and Theology

In 'The Theology of Genesis' (2012: 639), Joel Kaminsky describes the theology of the Bible as 'a raucous argument, spanning centuries' (p. 639). He suggests that 'one of the most interesting features of the theology of the Hebrew Bible is the willingness of the final redactors to incorporate diverse and even seemingly contradictory theological ideas within a single text', and that this has inspired later readers, 'perhaps more so in Jewish tradition than in Christianity', to argue with the text and with one another. Although Kaminsky's comments address the Bible generally, they are especially true of Genesis – Kaminsky's primary focus in the essay. Many of the literary features of Genesis contribute to making it a site of contestation. For example, Chapter 1 of this book explored theories (themselves contested) about the composition history of Genesis, highlighting the large number of places and times from which the materials included in Genesis are thought to have come, while Chapter 2 explored the various ways in which Genesis functions in its multiple literary contexts, and how consideration of those contexts helps to shed light upon meaning in Genesis. Indeed, Kaminsky opens his essay by suggesting that one of the best ways in which Genesis' theological significance can be explored is by 'probing its connection to the other four books of the Torah' (2012: 635).

A further feature of Genesis that contributes to the contestation within it is its extensive use of narrative. Even if today's readers, especially Christian, have a tendency to look to the Bible for guidance and instruction, they must admit that the OT, in particular, contains very little in the way of abstract analysis or statement of theological truths. Even the law, or 'instruction', is embedded in narrative. This, too, is true of Genesis. Most of Genesis is comprised of stories. This should not be taken to suggest that Genesis is interested more in entertainment than in communicating meaning. Stories may be profound bearers of meaning. Indeed, they could be said to be pregnant with meaning – pregnant, because the potential of the meaning they carry must be realized through interpretation. Each time a story is interpreted new meaning may emerge. This makes story both an ideal vehicle for the communication of elusive truths about the divine and a vehicle that must necessarily be generative of plural and contested meaning.

No single chapter of a study guide could hope to do justice to the many, and contested, themes and theological underpinnings of Genesis. My assumption in organizing this chapter is that Genesis expresses its theologies through narratives that can be more or less conveniently categorized by theme. Where particularly theological elements arise, I will highlight them. My proposed categories for the discussion of themes are designed to draw out elements of the contestation and 'raucous argument' that I've already referred to.

Creation/Uncreation

Genesis opens with two stories of creation (Gen. 1–2:4a and 2:4b–3), in which Yahweh, Israel's God, is presented as ultimate creator. These are origins stories, written to facilitate Israel's project to explore and establish her identity, and so to become the foundation of her hopes for the future. These stories of creation are not the OT's only origins stories, however, and comparison of these stories with other origins traditions is instructive. The other primary origins story in the OT is Exodus' account of the beginnings of the nation of Israel. In this story, Yahweh hears the suffering of the Israelites, rescues them from slavery, gives them land and law and elects them as Yahweh's own nation. There are other origins stories in the OT – for the Books of Chronicles, for example, real history begins only with the monarchy – but creation and exodus are the two primary origins accounts. Within the OT the two exist together in tension. Some books (typically Priestly, broadly speaking) look to Genesis' creation accounts for grounding of identity, while others (typically Deuteronomistic, broadly speaking) look to the Exodus salvation history for grounding of identity. A good example of the distinction between the two is found in the two accounts of the Ten Commandments (or 'Ten Words'), in Exodus and Deuteronomy. The two accounts are almost identical, but whereas Exodus 20 explains its injunction to observe the Sabbath through reference to creation (Exod. 20:8-11), Deuteronomy 5 appeals to the exodus experience (Deut. 5:12-15).

The Exodus account sees the beginning of history in the creation of the nation of Israel, through the adoption of her national God, Yahweh. Exodus is therefore a national story, in which Israel is conceived, and lives, among other nations (and empires) and their gods. Genesis does not explain Israel's origins in these terms. For Genesis, Yahweh is the creator of all there is – of the heavens and Earth. Yahweh is the God of all peoples, whether or not Yahweh is known by them, and whether or not they grant Yahweh their allegiance. There might be other divine bodies (e.g. Gen. 1:26 hints at the notion of a divine council, of which Yahweh is chair), but Yahweh is author of all. Whereas Exodus is a particularist story of origins, therefore, Genesis' creation accounts are universalist. Creation is not a national story, as in Exodus, but an international story, in which attention happens to be focused on a particular chosen family. In terms of the formation of identity, the creation tradition has important implications, both for understanding Yahweh and Yahweh's people. Yahweh is the author and deity of all people and of all created life. Genesis goes on to tell of Yahweh's choice of Abraham's family, but this choice is arguably as much about facilitating Yahweh's relationship with all people as it is about establishing a special bond with the descendants of Terah. In fact, the relationship set up in the creation accounts in Genesis is tri-partite. Creation is about the relationships between the creator God Yahweh, Yahweh's creation Earth and Yahweh's creation humanity.

Genesis' creation accounts are widely considered to have been influenced by the origins accounts, or 'cosmogonies', of Israel's neighbours in the Ancient Near East. In particular, the concept of a single, universalist, God was likely encouraged by traditions of similar supreme Mesopotamian deities, such as Marduk (Babylon) or Ahuramazda (Persia), which the Israelites would have encountered during the Babylonian exile. In this regard, the authors of the Genesis creation narratives can be understood to have been aspirational. In other words, in their identity-building they aspired to resemble not only their surrounding nations (with their national gods) but the empires to whom they were subject (who presented their gods as universal). Just as important as the similarities between Israel's cosmogony and those of her neighbours, however, are the differences between them. In fact, these differences are crucial keys to understanding what is distinctive about Israel's creation theology. The single biggest difference is to be found in Genesis' depiction of a single creator God. Even though other nations and empires had developed the notion of a single supreme god over time, their origins stories, written anything up to 1,000 years prior to the composition of Genesis 1–3, typically feature multiple divine characters, who are depicted as warring amongst themselves in pursuit of power. The Genesis creation stories, conversely, locate all power in a single God – Yahweh. There is thus no need for tension or violence between deities, so that Gen. 1–2:4a, in particular, is eirenic – all is goodness. There are further important differences in relation to the depiction of humans. In the Mesopotamian accounts, human beings tend to be created to be servants of the gods, running and maintaining their mythical temple precincts. In Genesis, human beings are not conceived as creatures made to tend to the needs and whims of their creator. Rather, Gen. 1:26-27 points to the near-divinity of humans, made in Yahweh's own image. Human beings are not given a purpose as such in Genesis 1, unless it is to bear the divine image and to procreate (i.e. to continue Yahweh's creative work). Some scholars have argued that the 'problem' of the near-divinity of humans is what drives Gen. 2:4b–3, a story in which humans gain knowledge, thus requiring that they be denied immortality, so that the distinction between humans and gods might be maintained with clarity. In Genesis 2–3 humans *are* given a job, as in the Mesopotamian cosmogonies, but they are made to serve not the gods but Yahweh's creation (Gen. 2:5, 15, 20), as Amanda Beckenstein Mbuvi (2016) maintains.

I have compared the Genesis creation accounts with the Exodus story and with other ANE cosmogonies. It is also instructive to compare them with one another. The Elohim of Gen. 1–2:4a is a transcendent, all-powerful God who creates principally through the spoken word. To be sure, there has been much discussion over centuries about precisely what 'creation' involves in Gen. 1–2:4a. Within Christianity especially, the idea of creation *ex nihilo* (out of nothing) has been influential. This is the idea that Elohim began to create in a context of the absence of matter. Alternative approaches have pointed to the elements that v.2 indicates were already present when Elohim began to create – the darkness, the deep waters and the Earth that was a formless void (*tohu wabohu* in Hebrew). In these approaches, Elohim's actions can be understood to comprise an 'ordering' or 'fashioning' of a pre-existing chaos. One highly suggestive recent approach is that of Ellen van Wolde (2009), who has argued, with appeal to the verb *br'* ('to create') in v.1, that Elohim's initial action was to 'cut off' Earth from the heavens, with which it had previously been contiguous. This idea has the merit of fitting well with the drawing of distinctions between deities and mortals already discussed, even if not all scholars have been persuaded that van Wolde's treatment of the verb is well-supported.

The form and language of Gen. 1–2:4a contribute significantly to its depiction of Elohim's creative activity (however it is defined). Genesis 1 is highly ritualized and repetitive. It has a carefully balanced structure. The action is divided into a succession of 'days', in each of which an account of new creation or 'ordering' or 'separation' is tempered by a (largely) uniform patterning of language. Further patterns are built between the days and the objects of their creative activity. The mood is peaceful, majestic and highly ritualized. It has been argued that the depiction of creation in Genesis (like that in other ANE cosmologies) is representative of the structure of the Jerusalem Temple. At every stage Elohim pronounces the new creative step taken to be 'good'. At the close of the sixth day, when the creative work is complete, Elohim observes it and sees that it is 'very good'. The text is opaque with respect to the question whether it is the creation of human beings on Day Six that is 'very good' (v.31) – thus arguably elevating humanity above other elements of creation – or whether the superlative refers to the totality of Elohim's creation, meaning that human beings (unlike other living creatures – see v.25) do not receive a specific notice of the divine recognition of their goodness at all.

Despite the fact that a number of scholars have argued that Gen. 1–2:4a is best understood as the work of 'H' or a 'Holiness School' (rather than of P in a more general sense), this first creation story does not pronounce creation, generally, to be 'holy'. Only one element of the first creation account is pronounced to be 'holy', and that is the seventh, or 'sabbath', day (Gen. 2:3). On this day Elohim rests, following the completion of the creative work. Links between this account and other 'sabbath' materials in Exodus and Leviticus make Gen. 2:2-3 important in establishing a theology of divine imitation. Human beings should rest from their work for one day a week, just as Elohim rested on the seventh day. Leviticus 25 goes further, requiring that the land, also, should observe a 'sabbath', and that every fifty years a 'sabbath of sabbaths' (or 'jubilee') be observed. For H, the failure of the land to observe its sabbath (a failure in which humans are implicated) is made the reason for the success of the Babylonian attack on Jerusalem and the exile (Lev. 26:34-35, 43). Elohim removed the Israelites from the land in order that the land might be able to observe the sabbaths it had missed. However, the failure of Genesis 1 to pronounce all creation 'holy' is not at odds with the theology of H, but rather in line with it. For H, holiness is aspirational. Earth, plants, birds, fish, animals and humans become holy through the observance of Torah. Gen. 1–2:4a, then, performs many functions, some of which are about explaining the origins of the world, and some of which are profoundly theological in other respects, including the setting out of the foundational stories that support the theology that shaped Priestly ideology, as most clearly articulated in a Triteuch comprising Genesis, Exodus and Leviticus (see Chapter 2).

The second creation account, found in Gen. 2:4(b)–3, is different from the first in many respects. Where the first account is universalist, grand and ritualized, the second is particular and intimate, and told in the style of a folk-story. (Note that the second account can still be described as 'universalist' in the sense that although it focuses its attention on individual characters, those characters are presented as proto-humans, rather than as proto-Israelites.) Further, the Yahweh Elohim of the second story is very different from the Elohim of the first. Yahweh Elohim is an imminent, even anthropomorphized, God (i.e. one who is presented in human guise), who walks in the garden, speaks and negotiates with its resident creatures, and creates by hand from the dust of the ground. In contrast to the first account, not everything is 'good' in this second story. There is a prompt for creation here, which is a lack of rain and of a creature to serve the ground (Gen. 2:5). This lack is soon rectified, but the creation of the human (*adam*) to serve the earth (*adamah*) creates a problem of its own. (Note the careful, and significant, wordplay, which serves to build important connections.) For the first time in Genesis, something is pronounced to be 'not good'. It is 'not good' that the *adam* should face the responsibility for serving the *adamah* alone (v.18). In this second story the animals and birds are created by Yahweh Elohim for the purpose of rectifying this second lack. None, however, is judged by the *adam* to be suitable for the task. It is not until a second *adam* (this time a woman, an *ishsha*) has been created from the first (who is now identified as a man, an *ish*) that the *ish* is satisfied that an appropriate partner has been found. The problems, however, *really* begin with the creation of the second human. Too often, particularly within Christianity, these problems have been laid at the feet of the second human, Eve, and, consequently, at the feet of the 'daughters of Eve' over millennia. The problems that ensue in the story, however, are not caused by one gender or the other, but rather by the challenging realities of relationship. When Genesis 3 is read in the context of the rest of the book, it becomes apparent that Genesis 3 announces one of the book's most prevalent themes – the ability (or inability) of humans to live together in peace. There is more about this below.

I would like to mention in passing one further area in which Genesis 2 has received attention that may be considered unwarranted, before moving on to Genesis 3. Many interpreters have taken the view, encouraged particularly by v.24, that gender complementarity is a core theme of Genesis 2. They argue that as the character found to be an appropriate helper-partner for the man was a woman, the authors of Genesis 2 intended to address the subject of marriage, and to legislate for heterosexual and against same-sex marriage. The argument is far too complex and fraught for it to be possible to do it justice here – very senior scholars have expressed markedly different views – save to say that I have argued elsewhere (Warner 2017) that the editors intended to address a very different moral issue (one with greater relevance to their own time), and not in a manner designed either to prescribe or to proscribe any particular sexual expression.

Creation/**Uncreation**

I have headed this discussion 'Creation/Uncreation'. It has been argued (Blenkinsopp 2011) that 'Creation, Uncreation and Recreation' could be identified as *the* theme of the opening chapters of Genesis (and more generally of the Primeval History, Genesis 1–11). Genesis 3 tells the story of the events that take place in the garden, leading to the expulsion of the first two humans – a kind of 'un-creation'. I have already mentioned one of the principal themes of the story – that of immortality. Some commentators suggest that Genesis 3 is the story of humankind's loss of immortality. In truth, humankind never possessed immortality at the outset, and so couldn't 'lose it', strictly speaking, as James Barr has argued (1993). The problem of immortality arose only once the humans had eaten from the tree of the knowledge of good and evil, which Adam had been instructed by Yahweh Elohim not to do in Gen. 2:16-17. Once the fruit had been eaten, and humans had attained god-like knowledge, they could not be allowed to eat *also* of the tree of life, thereby attaining god-like immortality, and so Yahweh Elohim exiled them from the garden.

Another approach, often regarded as 'traditional' within Christianity, maintains that Genesis 2–3 is the story of 'The Fall'. Proponents of this view have read the story though a particular Pauline lens, to interpret it as one in which God's glorious plans for the world and for humankind are thwarted when humans disobey God's rule by eating the fruit. This interpretation has been enormously influential, especially, as noted, among Christians. The

'Fall' interpretation is not, however, typical of Jewish approaches. Kaminsky (2012: 640), for example, writes:

> For centuries, Christians have read Genesis 3 as the story of the 'Fall of Man' .... This interpretation gave rise to the widespread theological doctrine of original sin. In such a reading, humans fell from a perfect state to a sinful one on the basis of a single error. However, an examination of Gen 3–11 indicates that it contains a series of linked narratives that describe the ongoing corruption of human beings and God's attempts to remedy this situation. There is little evidence to suggest that Gen 3 marks a complete change in the divine-human relationship.

The authority traditionally assigned to 'The Fall' interpretation has been challenged by numerous alternative readings. An example is the reading of feminist scholar, Lyn M. Bechtel. Bechtel argued (1995) that Gen. 2:4b–3:24 is a myth of human maturation. She posited the garden as a place in which the man and woman could grow from infancy towards maturity, and the transgression with the apple as an inevitable exercise in boundary-testing. In Bechtel's reading, God is presented as a benevolent but over-protective parent, who reluctantly recognizes that adolescents approaching adulthood must be allowed to leave, or even be pushed from, the protection of the parental nest, and barred from returning.

Further approaches to interpretation of the story have been opened up by new dating models, especially European, which allow readers to imagine the implications of a dating of this story *after* the destruction of Jerusalem. Even so, to date there have still been surprisingly few readings of Genesis 2–3 as an allegory of the Babylonian Exile. One such is that of Cynthia Edenburg (2011: 162):

> As others recently have noted, the recurring crime-punishment-exile theme in these narratives [Genesis 2–4] foreshadows the structure of the Deuteronomistic History. The man was created outside the garden and was placed within it by YHWH, but he was banished from the garden and from YHWH's immediate presence after breaking the single condition incumbent upon him. The paradise story thus plotted roughly parallels the DtrH in which YHWH takes the people from Egypt and brings them into the land, which they conditionally possess and then lose after repeatedly breaking their treaty with YHWH.

Edenburg argues that 'there is justification for viewing Genesis 2–4 as opening a thematic *inclusio* that ends with the description of the Babylonian conquest and exile in 2 Kgs 24:1 – 25:21'. In other words, Edenburg is suggesting that Genesis 2–4 can be read as the introduction to the grand story to which 2 Kings 24–25 is the conclusion. O'Connor (2018: 71) takes a similar approach, describing Genesis 3 as a disaster story that can be dubbed 'refraction of trauma'. Despite its 'mythic setting in time before time', she writes, 'intimations of Judah's history appear in it'.

In O'Connor's approach, Genesis 3 deals not only with 'creation' and 'uncreation' but also with 'recreation'. She sees Genesis 3 as a story of a distant past written to encourage hope for the future (2018: 72):

> Like Adam and Eve, the Judeans faced a world fraught with struggles, alienation, and loss. They needed an etiology of their own catastrophe, an interpretation of its causes, and an understanding of how they could go forward. Genesis 3 provides one explanation of disaster. Humans disobey God and God punishes them. This perspective helps theologically because it says that the divine-human relationship is not severed nor is God a powerless being. Such an explanation suggests that they may survive with help from God, with animal skins replacing fig leaves to cover their nakedness and provide protection. God does not abandon Adam and Eve but helps them survive.

Promise/Impossibility

The promises made by Yahweh to Abraham (or 'Abram', as he is called prior to Gen. 17:5) and to his descendants are, like Yahweh's creative acts, among the most readily recognized themes of Genesis. I have already written about the way in which the divine promises contribute to Genesis' function of generating hope for Israelites at a time when hope seemed to be in short supply. The promises take various forms, which are not always easily distinguishable. Some passages refer simply to 'promises'. Other passages place promises in the context of covenant-making narratives. In still other passages, promises are characterized using the language of 'oath'. Examples of all three are given below. One perhaps surprising feature shared by all, however, is that none is embedded very deeply in the text. What I mean by this is that all of these promises, covenants and oaths are found in passages of Genesis usually considered 'additional', 'redactional' or relatively 'late'. As Rendtorff influentially argued (1990), and as I noted already in Chapter 2, the promises appear to have been overlaid upon an already existing narrative. One indicator of this is that they do not always agree entirely with the surrounding narrative. For example, while Abraham is often presented as a paragon of faith or of Torah observance in promise material, the surrounding narrative presents him as a far more ambiguous character, whose behaviour is inconsistent – at times radically obedient and at others self-serving. Of course, even referring to Abraham as Torah-observant is anomalous in a narrative situated in a time before the Torah was given to Moses. What this suggests is that while 'promise' may be an important theme for Genesis, it was not a theme of Genesis' earliest forms, but may rather belong to the structural framework that holds Genesis together.

Promise

The very opening of Abraham's story features divine promise. Jean Louis Ska (2009) has described the divine promise to Abram in Gen. 12:1-4a as 'Israel's birth-certificate'. The passage functions as an opening of the Abraham Cycle, but also, arguably, of the Pentateuch, or even of the entire OT. O'Connor (2018: 189) suggests, 'It depicts in microcosm Israel's relationship with God, who pledges to make a people of them by giving them progeny, blessing, honor and land.' Yahweh appears to Abram (who, it is important to note, was already on the move in any event) and tells him to 'go!' to a land that Yahweh would show him (note that this instruction matches the divine instruction to Abraham to 'go!' to Mount Moriah in Genesis 22). This instruction is followed by a series of promises to Abram. Even though the instruction to go (leaving behind Abram's country, kindred and father's house) is followed by a set of promises, the promises are not stipulated as being conditional upon Abram's obedience. The point is moot because Abram does, in fact, go.

The promise of *progeny* is implicit in the first promise, to make of Abraham a 'great nation'. This same promise is later made about Jacob (Gen. 46:3, also in connection with a travel directive), Moses (Exod. 32:10) and Ishmael (twice, Gen. 17:20 and 21:18), but, strikingly, never Isaac. Elsewhere, the phrase 'great nation' is used of Israel (Deut. 4:6; 26:5). Progeny had already been announced as a preoccupation of Genesis in Gen. 1:28, and it is reflected here in the first promise to Abraham. Further, 'progeny' can be considered the foremost of the promises in the sense that the fulfilment of other promises is dependent upon fulfilment of the promise of progeny. Without offspring, for example, the promises of gifts of 'all the land of Canaan' (Gen. 17:8), 'this land' (Gen. 24:7), 'all these lands' (Gen. 26:4) and 'the land' (Gen. 35:12) to the offspring of Abraham, Isaac and Jacob is meaningless. Further promises of offspring include those found in Gen. 13:16, 17:2-8 and 16, 18:14 ('a son'), 21:12 and 22:15-18 (all Abraham), 26:4 and 24 (Isaac), 28:3 and 14 (Jacob) and 48:19 (Ephraim).

Promises to *bless* the ancestors and their offspring can be found throughout Genesis. The blessings promises made to Abram in Gen. 12:2-3 are, nevertheless, unique in some respects. The promise to make Abram's name great in v.2, for example, is unmatched in Genesis, but echoes a promise to David in 2 Sam. 7:9. Further, the motif of blessing those who bless Abraham and cursing those who curse him is echoed in the Pentateuch only in the Balaam story of Numbers 22–24. In the theology of D (and also H) blessings follow on from observance of Torah, while curses follow failures of Torah observance (Leviticus 26; Deuteronomy 28). The story (or history) of the Abrahamic family in Genesis, on the other hand, opens with an unconditional (subject to what I've already said about the direction 'go!') promise of blessing, to a character about whom the reader has been told nothing that might suggest to her that Abraham's divine favour has been in any way earned.

The promise of blessing in Gen. 12:2-3 is taken one step further in Gen. 12:3b: 'and in you all the families of the earth shall be blessed.' This is the first of five statements in Genesis of what has sometimes been termed the 'nations blessing promise'. The substance of this promise is difficult to pin down. In the most general sense, Abram is promised that all other families will somehow be blessed in or through him (or through his descendants). Further instances of this 'nations blessing promise' are found in Gen. 18:18, 22:18, 26:4 (Isaac) and 28:14 (Jacob). Details of the promise differ subtly in each iteration. For example, some speak of 'all the nations of the earth' and some of 'all the families of the earth', some use a more passive form of the form of the verb 'to bless' and some a more reflexive form, and in some instances the families/nations will be blessed in or through the ancestor to whom the promise is expressed, and in others, in or through his offspring. Although there is little scholarly agreement about the exact meaning of this group of promises, there is one outstanding and crucial question. Is the focus of this blessing on Abraham (and his offspring), so that it is a further statement of his blessed stature (i.e. he is so blessed that his blessedness will spill over to even impact non-Israelites), or is it a statement of divine interest in the blessedness of non-Israelites (in respect of whom Abraham and his descendants will take on the role of mediators, conduits or 'priests')? There is currently no consensus about the answer to this question. Carr (1996, and in subsequent work), for example, maintains that it is the former. I have argued, along with others (Grüneberg 2003; Noonan 2010), that it is the latter.

Promises of the bestowal of *honor* (to adopt O'Connor's term) are implicit in each of the promises in Gen. 12:2-3, although I have just raised a question about whether the 'nations blessing promise' is, in truth, a promise directed towards Abram's *honor*, or his vocation. I suggest that this is an important question. The phrase 'all the nations of the earth' appears in only one other place in the Pentateuch – the opening of Deuteronomy 28, that is, Deuteronomy's statement of the blessings and curses that will follow upon observance or non-observance of the Torah. Deut. 28:1 says, 'If you will only obey the Lord your God, by diligently observing all his commandments that I am commanding you today, the Lord your God will set you high above *all the nations of the earth*.' It is possible that the nations blessing promise in Genesis uses this same small phrase, 'all the nations of the earth', in order to disagree with Deuteronomy – suggesting that the relationship between Israel and the nations should not be one of comparative status, as in Deut. 28:1, but of comparative vocation, so that Israel is not placed higher than the nations but is rather given a vocation to serve them.

In order to complete this line of argument, it is worth noting that while three of the iterations of the nations blessing promise (Gen. 18:18; 22:18 and 26:4) use the phrase 'all the *nations* of the earth', the other two, including Gen. 12:3, use instead 'all the *families* of the earth'. This phrase, too, appears in only one other place in the Old Testament – Amos 3:2: 'You only have I known of *all the families of the earth*; therefore I will punish you for all your iniquities.' The subject of this verse is once again the consequence of the election of Israel. This time Yahweh's choice of Israel leads not to status but to increased punishment. Gen. 18:18 alludes strongly to Amos 3:2. Once again, a corrective tendency in the use of the phrase can be perceived in the nations blessing promise. The promise of blessing to Abraham's family are not, or not principally, about privileging them over other families but rather about charging and equipping Abraham's family to extend Yahweh's blessing to all peoples.

Finally, promises of *land*, too, are found throughout Genesis. The first is found in Gen. 12:7, followed by another in 13:14-18. In the Abraham Cycle alone, further statements of a land promise are found in Gen. 15:8, 18 and 17:8, and hinted at in Gen. 22:17. In Gen. 26:3-4 Yahweh promises Isaac that he and his descendants will be given not only Canaan but 'all these lands'. Jacob, meanwhile, is made a promise of land in Gen. 28:4, 13 and 35:12. Some of these promise texts are found in covenant-making narratives, and some use the language of 'oath'. Both are addressed below.

Of course, a land promise tradition is prominent also in the other books of the Pentateuch, while Joshua and Judges tell of the (partial) fulfilment of this divine promise. The Deuteronomistic History, meanwhile, can be read as the story of the loss of the land so promised. The land promise tradition(s) in Genesis, however, are different from the promises in these other books. They offer a 'new' (or old) tradition of a divine land gift to the ancestors (rather than to the exodus generations) that remains 'unsullied' or 'unthwarted' by Israel's failures that led to the need for Yahweh's punishment of Israel, delivered at the hands of the Babylonians.

The land promise(s) found in Genesis differ from those found in the rest of the Pentateuch in a number of important respects. For example, the scope of the land included within the promises in Genesis 15 and 26 is far greater than that of the land promises of Exodus–Deuteronomy. Further differences relate to the nature of the promise in Genesis. The land promise material outside Genesis is generally located in broadly Deuteronomistic text, and uses Deuteronomistic language to convey a D-flavoured concept of the 'possession' of land. Central to the concept of possession in D is the idea of 'exclusivity' – the possession of land in D implies the right, and even the responsibility, to remove others, including former owners, from it. The 'Conquest' narratives of Joshua and Judges tell of Israel's exercise of this responsibility. In Genesis, however, most (or even all) of the land-promise texts are either broadly Priestly or post-Priestly. The Priestly concept of possession of land (shared by P and H) is different from that of D. It stresses that the land remains the property of Yahweh, who grants the right to live in the land and enjoy it (the technical term is 'usufruct') to any and all chosen by Yahweh. Part of the outlook of P (and H), then, is that the recipients of a divine land gift may live in the land that has been gifted to them, alongside others to whom Yahweh has seen fit to 'give it' (Wöhrle 2010). This outlook is stated briefly in Lev. 25:23: 'The land shall not be sold in perpetuity, for the land is mine; with me you are but aliens and tenants.' Priestly texts (and some post-P texts) within Genesis reflect P's land theology through injunctions to Abraham and his family to live in the land 'as aliens'. Indeed, when Abraham approaches some Hittites in Genesis 23, seeking to buy land to bury Sarah, he introduces himself to them in precisely the language of Lev. 25:23. The picture conjured by Genesis, of a proto-Israelite family, living in close proximity to peoples of other families and nations, in a land that Yahweh has given them, reflects the theology of P. It is also reflective of the society of post-return Judah, as Nihan (2007) has observed. There is more about this below in discussion of the themes of peace and conflict.

Covenant

Genesis contains three covenant traditions – two Priestly and one non-Priestly. The two Priestly traditions concern covenants associated with Noah (Genesis 9) and Abraham (Genesis 17). The non-P covenant is made with Abram (Genesis 15). Many, although by no means all, of the promises recorded in Genesis are associated with these covenants. The covenants differ markedly in nature. For example, the Noah covenant extends not only to Noah and his descendants but to all living creatures. The term of the Noah covenant is extensive (eternal), while the substance of the Noah covenant is remarkably limited: 'that never again shall all flesh be cut off by the waters of a flood, and never again shall there be a flood to destroy the earth' (Gen. 9:11). The Noah covenant has a sign – the rainbow. The Priestly Abraham covenant, meanwhile, is more limited in its addressees – Abram himself in Gen. 17:4 and Abraham and his offspring (who are defined broadly in Genesis 17) in 17:7. P's Abraham covenant is for the same term as the Noah covenant (i.e. eternal – v. 7), but it encompasses a far broader series of promises, including promise representing all of the categories discussed above. Its sign is circumcision.

A further Abraham covenant is found in Genesis 15. It is not recognizably Priestly, but its provenance remains elusive. Genesis 15 defies classification according to the terms of the Documentary Hypothesis. Traditionally, it has been considered non-Priestly and *pre*-Priestly. Increasingly, however, especially in Europe, scholars have argued that it is *post*-Priestly and that it revises the Genesis 17 covenant. As seen already in Chapter 2, European scholars, in particular, have associated Genesis with the project to create a Hexateuch, and understand it to create an inclusion with Joshua 24. Some scholars, including Diana Lipton (1999), have argued, to the contrary, that Genesis 15 *resists* Joshua 24.

Outside Genesis, there are surprisingly few references to the Abraham covenants of Genesis 15 and 17, and little or no distinction made between them, although Priestly references, such as those in Exod. 2:24 and Lev. 26:42, are thought to allude specifically to Genesis 17. Of the few references to the Abraham covenant(s) found elsewhere in the OT, some refer to a covenant not just with Abraham but with 'Abraham, Isaac and Jacob' (Exod. 2:24; 2 Kgs 13:23; 2 Macc. 1:2) or, uniquely, in the case of Lev. 26:42, to the covenant(s) with Jacob, Isaac and Abraham. There are, however, no explicit narratives of covenant-making between Yahweh and Isaac or Jacob in Genesis, and there is currently no consensus about whether Genesis portrays the covenant being made anew with each of these male ancestors, or whether a single Abraham covenant is extended to his son and grandson. I take the latter view, as indicated already, on the basis of Genesis texts in which the imagery of royal succession is adopted for the purpose of the depiction of the extension of the covenant (and its associated promises) from father to son.

Oath

Gen. 22:15-18 and 26:3-5, which are not covenant passages, clothe the land promise in the language of divine oath. This is clearest in 26:3, where, in the context of a land promise, Yahweh tells Isaac that Yahweh will fulfil the oath Yahweh swore to Abraham. There is no narrative describing the swearing of a divine oath in the Abraham Cycle. However, the Angel of Yahweh alludes to the swearing of such an oath in the aftermath of the events at Moriah in Gen. 22:16. The two passages, Gen. 22:15-18 and 26:3-5, are so closely related to one another that most have concluded that the oath alluded to in 22:16 must be the oath expressly referenced in 26:3. In Chapter 2 I discussed the Deuteronomistic tradition of a divine land promise to the 'ancestors', expressed by oath. I also discussed the scholarship pointing to the likelihood that the 'ancestors' referenced by that tradition were not the ancestors of Genesis but rather the first exodus generation. It appears that those responsible for Gen. 22:15-18 and 26:3-5 wished to anchor the divine oath tradition in Genesis. Why? Such an exercise *could* have been about connecting Genesis with the rest of the Pentateuch. My conclusion, however, has been that the oath reference is connected with something else that happens in those two passages. I discussed this, too, in Chapter 2. In Gen. 26:3-5 Yahweh tells Isaac that the promises made to Abraham will be extended to Isaac *because* of Abraham's Torah observance. The links with Gen. 22:15-18 indicate that it is Abraham's actions at Moriah that are particularly in view. The impact of Gen. 26:3-5 is that the extension of the promise to Isaac is guaranteed partly by the divine oath and partly by Abraham's actions at Moriah (i.e. Abraham's willingness to sacrifice Isaac). To make a very long story short, the use of the oath motif is as much about reassurance that the promise will be kept by Yahweh as it is about setting out what those promises are.

Promise/**Impossibility**

The 'shadow side' of the promise theme in Genesis is that of 'impossibility'. One of the features of Genesis narrative, especially in Genesis 12–50, is the presentation of situations in which the continuation of life appears to be impossible (cf. Gen. 1:28). This feature announces itself immediately upon the introduction of Abram and Sarai. The only concrete piece of information the reader is given initially is that Sarai is barren (Gen. 11: 30). Only a few verses later, Abram is promised that he will become a great nation (Gen. 12:1-3). The tension between the reality and the promise becomes the driver of the Abraham Cycle. Initially, Abram's nephew Lot presents the only real hope for continuation of the Terahite family, but in Genesis 13 Abram and Lot separate and in Genesis 14 Lot is stolen by raiding kings. In Genesis 15, Abram airs his worries – 'Oh Lord God, what will you give me, for I continue childless' (15:2) – and promises of progeny and land are repeated to him. In Genesis 16, Abram and Sarai take matters into their own hands, using Sarai's Egyptian maid Hagar as surrogate, leading to the birth of Ishmael. In Chapters 17 and 18 promises of progeny are repeated, expanded and clarified. Abram is to become 'Abraham' – father not merely of a family or a 'great nation' but of many peoples. Sarai becomes Sarah, and Yahweh promises that none other than she will be the mother of Abraham's child. Both Abraham and Sarah laugh at the idea. In Genesis 19 and 20 the focus moves away from Abraham and Sarah to some degree, but the theme of impossibility continues. In Chapter 19 the Daughters of Lot produce children despite there being 'not a man on earth to come in to us in the manner of all the world' (Gen. 19:31). In Genesis 20 all the women of the house of a foreign king become temporarily barren, 'because of Sarah, Abraham's wife' (Gen. 20:18). Finally, Sarah gives birth to Isaac in Genesis 21.

Everything should be resolved, but now Abraham and Sarah have an ironic new problem – they have gone from having no heir to having two, and Sarah responds by sending Hagar and Ishmael away. At the commencement of Genesis 22 all appears, again, to have been resolved, but still the theme of impossibility has not been fully played out. Yahweh requires Abraham to kill Isaac, the son of promise and the necessary conduit for fulfilment of the promises. It is not until Abraham demonstrates his willingness to destroy the very thing that makes fulfilment of the promises possible that Yahweh relents and repeats the promises in their most emphatic form (22:15-18).

Of course, Sarah is not the only barren woman in Genesis. Rebekah is also barren prior to Isaac's prayer on her behalf. Rachel, too, is initially barren, and even Leah reaches a point when she is unable to bear more children (Amit 2012). The fecundity of the non-Abrahamite women in the narrative (Hagar, Lot's Daughters, Bilhah and Zilpah, and Tamar) places the barrenness of Sarah, Rebekah, Rachel and Leah in sharp relief. Nor is the inability to have children the only threat to the survival of Abraham's family in Genesis. Drought and famine are recurrent motifs in the narrative, beginning in Chapter 12 and reaching their apogee in the Joseph Story.

Why is 'impossibility' such a persistent theme in a story ostensibly about building future hope? The theme of impossibility will likely have struck a chord with the first audiences of Genesis, for whom 'impossibility' will have seemed to be a feature of their own future prospects. If Yahweh could achieve the impossible in the story, then perhaps, Genesis' earliest audiences might have reasoned, Yahweh could achieve the impossible in their lives also – finding a way ahead for a small and vulnerable group in a Jerusalem that lacked walls, temple, monarch and the hope of sovereignty.

Further motifs of the impossibility theme in Genesis 12–50 are (non-) fulfilment and delay. These, too, are likely to have represented worries and reality for the returned exiles. Other OT writings from the post-exilic period suggest that the returners waited for many years for a restoration of the Davidic monarchy, for example, only to have their hopes dashed in what represented a failure of earlier divine promises that there should always be a Davidic king. What good would new divine promises, like those made to Abraham, be if Yahweh had broken other promises? For that reason, asserting the new promise in Genesis would not be enough – the issue of fulfilment was one that also needed to be addressed. This appears to have been particularly a concern of Genesis 15. One of the many curiosities of Genesis 15 is that Abram is presented as both faithful (15:6) and uncertain – even wheedling. The chapter can be divided into two parts, the first dealing with the promise of progeny (vv. 1-6) and the latter with the promise of land (vv. 7-21). At the beginning of each section Abram complains and worries. In each section Yahweh responds, offering Abram representations designed to reassure him that he can rely on the promises. In the first section Yahweh shows Abram the stars in the sky as a representation of the number of his offspring. The response in the second section is more elaborate. Yahweh requires Abram to set up a ritual of sacrifice that echoes a description of a similar ritual in Jeremiah 34, as numerous scholars, including Van Seters (1975), Ha (1989) and Schmid (2010), have observed:

> … the officials of Judah, the officials of Jerusalem, the eunuchs, the priests, and all the people of the land who passed between the parts of the calf shall be handed over to their enemies and to those who seek their lives. Their corpses shall become food for the birds of the air and the wild animals of the earth.
>
> (Jer. 34:19-20)

In Gen. 15:17 it is Yahweh, represented by the smoking fire pot and flaming torch, that passes between the parts of the sacrificial animals. It is thus Yahweh, and not the Judahites (as in Jeremiah 34), who takes on the responsibility for, and risks associated with, maintenance of the covenant and its associated responsibilities (Warner 2018a). Here is an elaborate image designed to further Genesis' themes of promise and impossibility. It was apparently not enough that Genesis should present new divine promises for the cowed Israelites; Genesis had to present also encouragement and reassurance that these new promises would prove more reliable than the old ones.

Peace/Conflict

It has often been observed that Genesis is a peaceful, even eirenic, book. It lacks the violence of both its counterpart ANE cosmogonies and its fellow biblical books, including those found in the Pentateuch/Hexateuch. Abraham, for example, is depicted as an amiable and flexible (if sometimes somewhat hapless) immigrant, who sets about the task of moving and living among the peoples of other nations, and negotiating with their leaders. The radically respectful approach of Abraham to land purchase in Genesis 23 is a prime example of this. The Priestly outlook of Genesis, especially evident in the Abraham Cycle, promotes this approach, causing Genesis to differ from other books with a more Deuteronomistic outlook, which tend to foreground the need for strict separation between peoples, and the exclusivity of Yahweh's wishes for Israel, in respect to land, relationships and worship. Some of the differences between P and D understandings of ownership of land are set out in the discussion of the land promises above. Genesis' foregrounding of the Priestly approach to land possession functions to create a depiction of a society that is generally more inclusive than that represented in other pentateuchal books. Indeed, the difference can be seen to be stark when Abraham's congenial neighbour approach is contrasted with the calls in Exodus, Numbers and Deuteronomy for the expulsion or extermination of other peoples in order to facilitate Israel's eventual exclusive enjoyment of the land. Conceptions of land ownership are not the only thing that shape the general peacefulness of the Genesis narrative, however. The predominance of a Priestly world view also means that tensions around exclusivity of worship, and antipathy to the gods and worship accoutrements of non-Israelites, so prevalent in books in which a Deuteronomistic world view is prominent, are almost absent from Genesis.

This does not mean, of course, that tension, or even violence, are entirely missing in Genesis. Genesis 3 shines a light on the inevitability of conflict between human beings, and between human beings and God, while in Genesis 4 that conflict escalates and is expressed in fratricide. Conflict and violence are, then, presented as elements of the human condition almost from the very beginning. Nor is Yahweh depicted as an entirely peaceable deity, even if the internecine squabbling and battling of gods of the ANE cosmogonies is missing from Genesis. In Genesis 6–9 Yahweh, unhappy with the wickedness (6:5) or violence (6:11) of life upon Earth, determines to destroy all life, saving only one righteous man and his family, along with limited representatives of animals and birds. In our enthusiastic telling of this history as a children's story it is easy to miss the extraordinary recklessness and violence of the deity depicted in it. Genesis 12–50, too, contain stories of violence. Among these, the story of the monarchic raid on Lot in Genesis 14, Yahweh's destruction of Sodom and Gomorrah in Genesis 19, Esau's (supposed) murderous intentions towards Jacob following Jacob's deception in Genesis 27, the large-scale extermination of the Shechemites following Shechem's sexual assault of Dinah in Genesis 34 and the posited murder of Joseph by his brothers in Genesis 37 are foremost. Despite the violence of these stories, however, the general tenor of Genesis, when compared to the books following it, is remarkably peaceful.

One further reason for this is a tendency in Genesis narrative to seek for the resolution of tension and violence. Jacob and Esau, for example, reconcile and Jacob's fears in respect of his swindled brother are unrealized. Similarly, Joseph reconciles with his murderous brothers not once but twice, in Genesis 45 and 50. Jonathan Sacks (2015) traces the theme of the resolution of fraternal tension and violence in Genesis. Sacks argues that Genesis develops this theme from the depiction of a simple instance of fratricide in Genesis 4, through to a rich and multilayered account of the resolution of brotherly conflict in the Joseph Story. Not only intra-familial tensions are resolved, what's more. Genesis 26 is an often-overlooked account of the resolution of tensions between members of different ethnic groups. It is discussed in further detail below.

Further, Genesis recognizes and depicts conflict not only between humans but also between humans and Yahweh. One of the central stories of the Jacob Cycle, the story in which Jacob receives his new name, Israel, is found in Gen. 32:22-32. In the story, Jacob 'struggles' or 'strives' overnight with a stranger, and he prevails. The legacy of the struggle includes both blessing (32:29) and injury (32:31). Further, Jacob is given a new name, 'Israel', which means something resembling 'struggle' or 'striving' with God. This is the name, too, of Yahweh's chosen people, of course, so that the nation, Israel, is thus depicted by the story as one which struggles or strives with its God and is rewarded with blessing and injury. Struggle, or conflict, then, is represented by Genesis as the core of the relationship between Yahweh and Yahweh's chosen people, and therefore as the core of Israel's identity.

Peace/**Conflict**

More generally, then, Genesis is by no means averse to examinations of issues around violence and conflict. However, it tends to deal with these issues in a conscious and deliberate manner. Genesis does not tell stories of violence or war simply for the sake of reportage. Rather, as Sacks (2015) suggests, such stories are told for the purpose of weighing and evaluation. This approach in Genesis – of telling stories for the purpose of weighing and evaluating different options, or exploring different outlooks or conundrums – is not limited to treatment of stories of violent conflict. The authors of Genesis often wrote stories as case studies, including case studies of a legal nature (Warner 2018b). In such stories, two or more approaches to a single problem or situation are presented, with the narrator sometimes offering an opinion on the better approach, and sometimes not. These different approaches might be outlined within a single story, such as the story of the sexual assault of Dinah in Genesis 34 (discussed below). Sometimes they are outlined in two consecutive stories, such as the stories of the threats to Abraham's two sons in Genesis 21 and 22, or the stories of the sexual threats to, or sexual 'tests' of, Judah and Joseph in Genesis 38 and 39. Sometimes two or more stories, which might be separated by many chapters, address identical issues within the bounds of apparently different narrative contexts. Examples include the story of Noah and Ham in Gen. 9:18-29, the story of Lot's Daughters in Gen. 19:30-38 and the story of Tamar and Judah in Genesis 38. Even though each of these stories appears, on its face, to be substantially different from the others, they are joined by a complicated web of themes, circumstances and legal principles. In short, each story concerns sexualized contact between children (probably young adults) and their parents, initiated by the child, in a context of disaster or transgression. Yair Zakovitch (1993) influentially coined the term 'reflection stories' for such stories in Genesis, and argued for the interpretational possibilities that arise when they are read together.

In the remainder of this chapter, I discuss one single story and one group of stories that address the theme of conflict. The first is the story of the sexual assault of Dinah in Genesis 34. The second is a story that is told three times in Genesis about the conflicts that arise in the context of the sharing of land, found in Genesis 13, 21:22-34, and 26:12-35.

Genesis 34

In Genesis 34, violence erupts after a Hivite prince, Shechem, sexually assaults Dinah, the only named daughter of Jacob. The violence is instigated by two of Dinah's brothers, Simeon and Levi. Incensed by the attack on their sister, particularly at the hands of a non-Israelite ('because he had committed an outrage in Israel by lying with Jacob's daughter, for such a thing ought not to be done', v.7), Simeon and Levi trick the Hivites into circumcising their males, and then lead an attack on them during the recovery period. The attack is extremely violent. They kill all the males and take Dinah to safety. Subsequently their brothers, also in response to Dinah's humiliation, plunder the city of Shechem, capturing women and children, animals and possessions.

Jacob's response is different from that of his sons. Initially, upon hearing news of Shechem's 'defilement' of Dinah, Jacob is pensive. He resolves to wait until his sons return from their work in the fields before determining his response. Despite their anger, he allows time for discussion of the matter with Hamor, Shechem's father. Hamor pleads with Jacob and his family to allow his son to marry Dinah, and paints a picture of peaceful cohabitation, in which Jacobites and Hivites live alongside one another, trading together and intermarrying.

In the discussion, Jacob apparently allows his sons to take the lead. They appear to agree to Hamor's proposal on the condition that the Hivites become circumcised. If they will do so, Jacob's family will remain and allow the marriage of Shechem and Dinah. If not, Jacob's family will leave and live elsewhere, taking Dinah with them. The reader is told that in the discussion Jacob's sons speak deceitfully. Jacob does not speak or act again until after his sons' violence. He approaches Simeon and Levi and expresses regret at their actions. He tells them that their actions have 'brought trouble' upon him and made both him and his household vulnerable to future attack (v.30). The narrator gives Simeon and Levi the last word – 'Should our sister be treated like a whore?' (v.31) – neither recording Jacob's response nor offering his own.

Many commentators in recent years have read this story against the background of the 'foreign wives crisis' of the post-exilic period, described most vividly in Ezra and Nehemiah. The explicit discussion of intermarriage in the story suggests strongly that it responds, in one way or another, to that crisis. Where there has been disagreement amongst scholars, it has been about the nature of the response in Genesis 34. The majority of commentators have argued that Genesis 34 supports the opposition to the practice of intermarriage found not only in Ezra and Nehemiah but also in other books of the Pentateuch. The implication of this argument is that Simeon and Levi responded appropriately to Shechem's transgression of Israel's sexual laws. These scholars have tended to be critical of Jacob's role in the story, arguing that it presents him as weak or vacillating. A smaller number of commentators have, conversely, been critical of the actions of Jacob's sons. They argue that Genesis 34 intends not to support but to undermine opposition to intermarriage. They point to a disproportionality in Simeon and Levi's response, and note that the actions of their brothers contravene other provisions of Torah about the conduct of war. They note an element of hypocrisy in the conduct of Simeon, who, according to Gen. 46:10, had a child with a Canaanite woman, and they question the repeated use in the story of the word 'defilement', which is not a word applied by Torah to sexual assault of an unbetrothed woman.

I have argued something slightly different. Noting that each of these readings represents a valid interpretation of the text, I have argued that both are intentionally present in it, and that the authors of the story intended to present a conundrum about the appropriate response to unprovoked sexual attack, without resolving it. Should one respond with violence, upholding the honour of the shamed woman and her family? Or should one instead take a long-term and conciliatory view, bearing in mind one's vulnerabilities and the desirability of peaceful neighbourly relations? On this reading, both the attack upon Dinah and the resulting violence are relatively marginal elements of the story. Certainly, in the story itself, both are described with the minimum of fuss and detail. The real focus of the story, arguably, is the negotiation between the Jacobites and Hivites over terms by which they might live together peaceably, and the attitudes of both parties to that negotiation. Certainly, the larger part of the narrative is given over to this subject – usually a good indicator of a text's focus. The attack on Dinah, on this reading, is representative of the conflict that typically arises whenever humans (and particularly human of different ethnicities) live in close proximity. The Priestly outlook of Genesis, especially in the light of P's concept of land possession, contemplates precisely this sort of proximate living. The inclusion of Genesis 34 is an indicator that P is not entirely unrealistic in its promotion of its vision but understands its potential for conflict and even violence. Genesis 34 is a story that addresses the inevitability of such conflict and violence and raises questions about how it might best be managed.

Genesis 13, 21:22-34 and 26:12-35

These three stories are not sufficiently often recognized as a group. They follow immediately upon the three stories that have variously been described as 'the ancestress in danger' or 'wife-as-sister' stories in Gen. 12:10-20, 20 and 26:1-11. In each case, an account of the ancestor (twice Abraham and once Isaac) causing his wife to be vulnerable to the sexual attentions of a foreign king is followed (more-or-less) immediately by a story about the challenges of land-sharing.

Genesis 13 is an intra-familial story. After Abram and Sarai's encounter with Pharaoh in Gen. 12:10-20, Abram has been furnished with riches of animals and slaves (v. 16) and gold and silver (13:2). Upon his return from Egypt, he finds that the combined possessions of Abram and Lot are too great for them to live together, and that cohabitation is leading to strife between the herders of their respective livestock. The solution is for the two, Abram and Lot, to separate and share out the land between them. Following the separation, Abram receives divine promises of land and progeny.

Although the wife-as-sister account in Genesis 20 is divided from the land-sharing story in Gen. 21:22-34 by the accounts of the birth of Isaac and the expulsion of Hagar and Ishmael, the two belong together. The events of Gen. 21:22-34 arise as the direct result of those of Genesis 20. In Gen. 20:15

Abimelech presents his land to Abraham and invites Abraham to settle in it, wherever pleases him. Abimelech also offers Abraham wealth in the form of silver. In the intervening period of Isaac's birth and his early years, it appears that tensions have arisen between the Philistines and Abraham's household, impliedly still living in Philistine territory (21.34, cf. 21:32). Abimelech approaches Abraham, seeking some kind of non-aggression pact. He sees that God is with Abraham and wants Abraham to agree not to deal falsely with him or with his people. Abraham responds by telling Abimelech about tensions between himself and Abimelech's servants relating to a well. Abimelech denies any knowledge of this problem, but the two agree and swear an oath and make a covenant together.

In Genesis 26 there is no division between the stories, and both are included under the umbrella of a single chapter. The plot is very similar to that of both Genesis 20 and Gen. 21:22-34, except that Abraham and Sarah are replaced by Isaac and Rebekah, and the sexual threat to Rebekah is neutralized early in the story, so that the ancestress is never really placed in any great danger. Once again, the wealth of the ancestor is a factor, but this time Abimelech, troubled by tensions that develop between his herders and Isaac's servants, again around ownership of wells, tells Isaac to move away. Isaac does so, although the implication is that he does not move far. In Gen. 26:26 Abimelech (or Abimelech Jr?) again travels to visit the ancestor for the purpose of resolving the tensions between their peoples. There are some subtle differences at this point. The first is that this time Abimelech brings with him an adviser whose name, *Achuzzath*, echoes the Priestly term for possession of land, *achuzzah*, and who is arguably designed to remind readers of it. Second, Abimelech's request of Isaac is for something more like a peace treaty than a non-aggression pact. Once the two have sworn an oath and made a covenant, as in the Genesis 21 story, the text says that Abimelech and his retinue depart 'in peace'. This is one of the two places in the story where the word 'peace' is used. In no other Genesis narrative does the word appear more than once.

Scholars have debated for centuries why the 'wife-as-sister' story is told three times in Genesis. The three 'land-sharing' stories that follow them have, however, received relatively little attention. Most of the proposed solutions have been rooted in source-critical arguments. The land-sharing stories, however, suggest something different. A progression can be observed across the three stories, much as Sacks observed a progression across the stories of fraternal violence. As the stories progress, the focus upon the sexual catalyst for the development of tensions decreases, while the focus on the resolution of differences increases. In the first of the three stories the land-sharing difficulties are between family members (uncle and nephew) and they prove insoluble. The two divide the land between them and part company. In the second story the divisions are between different ethnic groups and they are resolved by means of an agreement to avoid aggression. The third story again involves an ethnic divide, but the parties are able to agree to coexist peacefully, rather than simply to avoid the expression of tensions through conflict.

There are some similarities of theme between these stories and Genesis 34. For both, the initial tensions are sparked by sexual encounter and there are attempts to regulate ongoing relationship through negotiation. Strikingly, there is evidence of allusion running between Genesis 26 and 34. Both articulate a concept of a divine enlargement of land that makes it possible for peoples of different ethnicities to live in it together (Gen. 26:22; 34:21) that is not found anywhere else in Genesis, and that is at odds with use of the Hebrew term 'to enlarge' elsewhere in the Pentateuch. There is a good argument to be made for considering Genesis 26 and 34 to be 'reflection stories' in the sense suggested by Zakovitch.

I have explored these stories at some length because together they give a strong indication of a theme in Genesis, 'conflict arising in the context of land-sharing', that is significant, but that is often overlooked.

As a final observation, it is important to reiterate that I have by no means identified or discussed all of the themes of Genesis. To do so would be beyond the scope of this study guide. What this chapter tries to do, instead, is to identify six of the foremost themes, with their theological underpinnings, and to show something of the ways in which these themes are in conversation and argumentation with each other.

References

Amit, Yairah. (2012), *In Praise of Editing in the Hebrew Bible: Collected Essays in Retrospect*, HBM, Sheffield: Sheffield Phoenix Press.

Barr, James. (1993), *The Garden of Eden and the Hope of Immortality*, Minneapolis, MN: Fortress Press.

Bechtel, Lyn M. (1995), 'Genesis 2.4B – 3.25: A Myth about Human Maturation', *JSOT* 20(67): 3–26.

Blenkinsopp, Joseph. (2011), *Creation Un-Creation Re-Creation: A Discursive Commentary on Genesis 1–11*, London: T&T Clark.

Carr, David M. (1996), *Reading the Fractures of Genesis: Historical and Literary Approaches*, Louisville, KY: Westminster John Knox Press.

Edenburg, Cynthia. (2011), 'From Eden to Babylon: Reading Genesis 2–4 as a Paradigmatic Narrative', in *Pentateuch, Hexateuch or Enneateuch: Identifying Literary Works in Genesis through Kings*, 155–69, AIL 8, Atlanta, GA: SBL.

Grüneberg, Keith N. (2003), *Abraham, Blessing and the Nations: A Philological and Exegetical Study of Genesis 12:3 in Its Narrative Context*, BZAW 332, Berlin: Walter de Gruyter.

Ha, John. (1989), *Genesis 15: A Theological Compendium of Pentateuchal History*, Berlin: Walter de Gruyter.

Kaminsky, Joel S. (2012), 'The Theology of Genesis', in Craig A. Evans et al. (eds), *The Book of Genesis: Composition, Reception, and Interpretation*, 635–56, VTSup 152, Atlanta, GA: SBL.

Lipton, Diana. (1999), *Revisions of the Night: Politics and Promises in the Patriarchal Dreams of Genesis*, JSOTSup, Sheffield: Sheffield Academic.

Mbuvi, Amanda Beckenstein. (2016), *Belonging in Genesis: Biblical Israel and the Politics of Identity Formation*, Waco, TX: Baylor.

Nihan, Christophe. (2007), *From Priestly Torah to Pentateuch*, FAT II 25, Tübingen: Mohr Siebeck.

Noonan, Benjamin J. (2010), 'Abraham, Blessing and the Nations: A Reexamination of the Niphal and Hitpael of ברך in the Patriarchal Narratives', *Hebrew Studies* 51: 73–93.

O'Connor, Kathleen M. (2018), *Genesis 1–25A*, Macon, GA: Smyth & Helwys.

Rendtorff, Rolf. (1990), *The Problem of the Process of Transmission in the Pentateuch*, trans. J.J. Scullion, JSOTSup 89, Sheffield: JSOT.

Sacks, Jonathan. (2015), *Not in God's Name: Confronting Religious Violence*, London: Hodder and Stoughton.

Schmid, Konrad. (2010), *Genesis and the Moses Story: Israel's Dual Origins in the Hebrew Bible*, trans. James D. Nogalski, Siphrut 3, Winona Lake, IN: Eisenbrauns.

Ska, Jean-Louis. (2009), 'The Call of Abraham and Israel's Birth-Certificate (Gen 12: 1-4a)', in *The Exegesis of the Pentateuch: Exegetical Studies and Basic Questions*, 46–66, FAT 66, Tübingen: Mohr Siebeck.

Van Seters, John. (1975), *Abraham in History and Tradition*, New Haven, CN: Yale University Press.

Van Wolde, Ellen. (2009), 'Why the Verb ברא Does Not Mean "to Create" in Genesis 1.1-2.4a', *JSOT* 34(1): 3–23.

Warner, Megan. (2017), 'Therefore a Man Leaves His Father and His Mother and Clings to His Wife: Marriage and Intermarriage in Gen 2:24', *JBL* 113: 269–89.

Warner, Megan. (2018a), *Re-Imagining Abraham: A Re-Assessment of the Influence of Deuteronomism in Genesis*, OTS 72, Leiden: Brill.

Warner, Megan. (2018b), 'What If They're Foreign?: Inner-Legal Exegesis in the Ancestral Narratives', in Mark G. Brett and Jakob Wöhrle (eds), *The Politics of the Ancestors: Exegetical and Historical Perspectives on Genesis 12–36*, 67–92, FAT 124, Tübingen: Moher Siebeck.

Wöhrle, Jakob. (2010), 'The Un-Empty Land: The Concept of Exile and Land in P', in Ehud Ben Zvi and Christophe Levin (eds), *The Concept of Exile in Ancient Israel and Its Historical Contexts*, 189–206, BZAW 404, Berlin: Walter de Gruyter.

Zakovitch, Yair. (1993), 'Through the Looking Glass: Reflections/Inversions of Genesis Stories in the Bible', *BibInt* 1(2): 139–52.

4

Reading Genesis in a Postmodern World

This final chapter explores newer approaches to reading and interpreting biblical text. Some of these, particularly in relation to Genesis, have risen in popularity because of the increasing complexity of applying historical-critical method to pentateuchal books. Most, however, reflect burgeoning interest in newer fields of enquiry, such as empire and postcolonial studies, trauma theory and ecology, or approaches that explore issues of identity and power through focus on gender, sexuality, ethnicity, disability and neurodiversity, for example. In general, interest in reader-response approaches, or those that explore dialogue between the text and the 'world in front of' the text, has grown exponentially, even if such approaches can also cross over with more historical or literary approaches. Few of these approaches are interested in isolating any single meaning as 'the' meaning of the text or in trying to identify authorial intention. More often, scholars employing these approaches wish to interrogate the biblical text against the measures of a given contemporary issue or school of thought, to draw new meaning out of the text, or to assess what the text has to say that speaks into that issue or school of thought, or perhaps to evaluate the text in the light of contemporary views and contexts.

There is not space in this chapter to consider all of these new approaches in detail, and even to try to name them exhaustively would likely be a thankless task. Those who wish to explore approaches to reading Genesis in more detail might like to consult Ronald Hendel's edited collection of essays on the subject, *Reading Genesis: Ten Methods* (2010). Instead, I have chosen five newer hermeneutical approaches, which I will introduce and discuss in relation to examples drawn from Genesis. Those chosen either have particular application to Genesis or are approaches that have been taken to

Genesis in recent years. In addition, at the end of each section I will apply the approach in question to a single sample text, Gen. 21:8-21. In this way I will try to convey how bringing a variety of fields of enquiry to the text as hermeneutical lens can shine light on elements of the text that are different in each case, or that have hitherto been overlooked or devalued.

Trauma-Informed Readings

The popularity of the use of trauma theory as lens for reading biblical text has grown enormously in recent years. Trauma theory itself is still in its infancy, having been developed in response to clinical treatment, first, of returned service women and men (especially from the Vietnam War), and then of victims of sexual abuse, both in childhood and as adults. David M. Carr's *Holy Resilience*, published in 2014, was one of the earliest extended English-language studies of the application of trauma theory to reading biblical texts. It was followed not long after by a collection of essays edited by Elizabeth Boase and Christopher Frechette titled *Bible through the Lens of Trauma* (2016), which remains a primary authority, although it has been followed by other collections and numerous articles, essays and monographs. Other related approaches have grown out of the 'trauma theory as lens' approach, including the use of 'resilience' and 'vulnerability' as lenses.

This study guide, itself, has been profoundly informed by trauma studies. From the beginning of the guide, I have encouraged readers to conceptualize Genesis as having been written and read by its earliest audiences in the wake of the trauma of the Babylonian exile. Despite the popularity of trauma theory as lens, however, there has been surprisingly little scholarly application of trauma theory to Genesis. Although Carr bases a good deal of his discussion in *Holy Resilience* on Genesis, and Kathleen O'Connor's two-volume Genesis commentary (2018/2020) takes trauma theory as one of its central foci, there has been surprisingly little in the way of extended reading of Genesis through the lens of trauma. It is likely that the relatively peaceful nature of Genesis (addressed in Chapter 3) has dissuaded scholars from attempting trauma-focused work on Genesis. Genesis does not focus on the suffering and violence of the Babylonian crisis. Indeed, because of its setting in the distant past, it does not even mention the crisis. Nevertheless, the fact that Genesis was (largely) written and compiled in its aftermath means that the trauma of the violent sacking of Jerusalem, the enforced migration of part of her population to Babylon and the dispiriting return, all make their mark on the text, even if they do not, for the most part, manifest in violent or war-like narrative. There are other ways in which the trauma experienced by Genesis' authors and earliest audiences is made manifest.

In the introduction to their collection of essays, Boase and Frechette (2016: 4) write that 'three dominant threads' inform the application of trauma studies to Bible text at present: psychology, sociology, and literary and cultural studies. They continue (2016: 13):

> In the turn to trauma as a hermeneutical lens, what is emerging is not a single methodological approach, but rather a heuristic framework. Through sensitivity to the nexus between historical events and literary representation, this framework has the capacity to bring into focus the relationship between the traumatic experience and both the production and the appropriation of texts. Fundamentally, a hermeneutics of trauma is attuned to the fact that language can encode and respond to traumatic experience in ways that correspond to the effects of trauma as well as to mechanisms of survival, recovery and resilience. Moreover, as already noted, the context of a trauma narrative may organize such language into narrative elements that are linear as well as non-linear, logical as well as imagistic. …
>
> When biblical scholars employ trauma hermeneutics to explore texts that have emerged out of contexts of trauma, they attend to the historical realities of traumatic violence and the disruptive and enduring impacts of those events on individuals and communities. In doing so, they are able to build upon the results of historical-critical approaches by accounting for features of the text that reflect psychological, cultural, and sociological impacts of traumatic events. Of particular interest are texts that have emerged from experiences of collective devastation, exile, or oppression.

In Chapter 3 I identified 'impossibility' as a theme of Genesis, and explored a range of texts that narrate stories in which there seems no possibility of a future. These included stories of the barrenness of many of the central women characters, and the recurrence of famine. In each case God overcomes the apparent roadblock and the characters are able to continue their own lives, to procreate and to continue their lines. The telling of such a story of 'impossibility' communicates to an audience living through apparently impossible times that God has responded in crises many times before, and will do so again. Stories of impossibilities overcome build hope. However, not all trauma narratives are told in order to build hope. They may take many approaches and perform many functions, such as standing witness to the horror, or hopelessness, of situations in which humans find themselves.

Trauma narratives may give expression to unspeakable emotions, or model any number of edifying or unedifying responses to situations or to God. They may rehearse injustices or insults, but in the relative safety of narrative.

O'Connor offers an attractive trauma-based insight into a story that has long puzzled readers. In Genesis 4, Yahweh prefers an offering presented by Abel to that presented by Cain. No reason is offered for the divine preference, but the consequences prove to be disastrous when Cain kills his brother. Scholars have long sought to exculpate Yahweh by offering explanations based on the content of each offering (about which the text is famously opaque). Others have simply deplored Yahweh's apparent capriciousness. No one has yet offered a universally satisfying 'meaning' for the story. O'Connor (2018: 80) provides not a 'meaning' as such but a trauma-informed observation about why such a story might be told, and why it might resonate with survivors of trauma:

> The Cain and Abel story reflects the dilemma of the nation's destruction under Babylon and why some survived, some were exiled and some died. For survivors and their offspring, the inscrutability of the divine choice of Abel may be a theological reflection after the fact, a search for explanation and comfort if the inscrutable God chose the survivors. Such theological reflections often emerge from tragic conditions where some few make it through alive but are unable to explain how that happened unless God chose them.

O'Connor presents the story as one that speaks to, and that has the capacity to ease, survivor guilt. Without the adoption of trauma as a lens, this insight may not have come to light.

Gen. 21:8-21

As this is the first of five readings of this passage, some introduction is warranted. In this passage, the divine promise of a son that would be Abraham and Sarah's own has been fulfilled. The problem that had driven the narrative ever since the close of Genesis 11 has been solved – Abraham has his longed-for heir. However, he finds himself with a new problem. Now he has two potential heirs instead of none. One is *his* eldest son, and the other is *Sarah's* eldest son. Abraham and Sarah, using their own initiative, had got themselves a son with the assistance of Sarah's Egyptian maidservant, Hagar. Ishmael, according to the text, was thirteen years old when Isaac was born. He had been their only child for many years.

Abraham's wife, Sarah, apparently does not cope well with the transition. She sees Ishmael 'playing' with her son Isaac. The verb translated as 'playing' here is the verb upon which Isaac's name is built. The implication is that Sarah sees Ishmael 'Isaacing' – displacing Isaac. She demands that Abraham 'cast out' Hagar and her son Ishmael, to ensure that Ishmael will not share in (what she sees as) Isaac's inheritance. Abraham is 'very distressed' (NRSV) by Sarah's demands, but God speaks to him, reassuring him, and urging him to do as Sarah asks. Abraham gets up early in the morning, gives Hagar some bread and water and sends her, along with Ismael, into the wilderness – presumably to die.

For most readers today the trauma of the story belongs (quite properly) to Hagar. She is the one who is sent away, with her child, into the wilderness. I will focus on Hagar and Ishmael in another reading, but for the moment I want to consider the situation from Abraham's perspective. Reading through the lens of trauma may begin, as was the case for O'Connor's reading of Genesis 4, with drawing parallels between a narrative and known events from the time when the story is likely to have been composed. A striking parallel to this narrative can be found in the accounts in Ezra and Nehemiah of the so-called 'foreign wives crisis', which led to the wholesale expulsion, or divorce, of foreign women taken as wives by Israelite men. Brett (2000: 61) suggests that Genesis 21 can be considered a 'political allegory' of those events. One can only imagine that the demand of the imperial governors in this regard (e.g. Ezra 10:11) would have been traumatic for the husbands as well as for their wives. To 'send away' or 'divorce' a woman in post-return Israelite society would have been to consign her to destitution if not to death. Nevertheless, Ezra 10:44 maintains that the Israelite men did as they had been directed and sent their foreign wives and children away.

Gen. 21:8-21 can be read as a story that reflects and responds to the experience of these husbands. In the story, Abraham is resistant to Sarah's wish to send away Hagar and Ishmael. A literal translation of the Hebrew text of Gen. 21:11 indicates that the idea was *exceedingly evil* to Abraham's eyes, on account of his son. (As indicated above, the NRSV translates the Hebrew to reflect a sense of 'distress' on Abraham's part, which is not necessarily the same thing.) Two things about this short verse are highly significant. First, and contrary to Genesis 22 (particularly vv. 2 and 16), which maintains that Isaac was Abraham's *only* son, Gen. 21:11 makes it clear that Ishmael was Abraham's son too. Second, Gen. 21:11 indicates that Abraham experienced strong emotional or moral reaction to Sarah's demand on Ishmael's account. One of the striking features of the Abraham Cycle as a whole is the lack of emotions and thoughts ascribed in it to Abraham, including, and perhaps especially, in Genesis 22. Gen. 21:11 is one of the very few places (if not the only place) in which the narrator gives the reader access to Abraham's inner world. To be sure, there are instances in which Abraham makes speeches that illuminate his thoughts or concerns, such as in the wife-as-sister stories of Genesis 12 and 20, or the two places in Genesis 15 in which Abram expresses his concern about fulfilment of the promise. However, Abraham does not speak here. Rather, the narrator recounts Abraham's internal response to Sarah's demand. And Abraham's response is dramatic. Sarah's demand seems *exceedingly evil* in Abraham's eyes. Not only does Gen. 21:11 contain a particle (i.e. a short word) of intensity ('exceedingly') but God repeats the verb 'to be evil' in Gen. 21:12, saying to Abraham, 'may you not do evil in your eyes on account of your son and your slave woman', but 'in everything that Sarah says to you, listen to her voice'. God goes on further, to reassure Abraham that Abraham's name would be carried on through the offspring of Isaac, and that Ishmael, too, would be blessed. At the end of the story God intervenes again to save Ishmael and his mother and to repeat promises to them directly.

How does this story look in the light of the experiences of male Israelites in the post-exilic period, pressured to expel foreign wives and children? The story indicates that Abraham was responding to forces outside his control. It was not his idea to get rid of his wife and child, but Sarah's. The harshness was all Sarah's. Abraham did not lose his moral compass. He recognized the great evil of what Sarah was demanding of him. Nevertheless, the guilt that might otherwise have weighed on him for going along with Sarah's plan was lifted from him as a result of God's support of it. Further, Abraham had received reassurance that taking this action would not negate the divine promise. Sons would come to him through Isaac, and Ishmael, too, would be the recipient of divine favour.

This is a story that would likely have spoken to the guilt and to the moral dilemma of Israelite males, pressured by Ezra to send away their foreign wives and children against their wishes. Abraham's concerns are likely to have reflected their own, that the order to send away their wives and children was morally wrong. The earliest readers are likely to have identified with Abraham, stuck, like them, in an impossible moral dilemma. At the same time, they might be thought to have been reassured that, in God's eyes, sending wives and children away was the right thing to do, regardless of their misgivings. It was right, the story suggests, to listen to Ezra's voice in this matter. Moreover, the earliest readers may have been reassured that God would care for the dismissed wives and children. They would not die but would be protected by God.

On this reading, Gen. 21:8-21 can be understood as another story, like the story of Cain and Abel in Genesis 4, told for the sake of assuaging a form of survivor's guilt.

Political Readings

In the opening line of their introduction to *The Politics of the Ancestors* (2018: 1), editors Mark G. Brett and Jakob Wöhrle write, 'The ancestral narratives of the book of Genesis have a decidedly political character.' They argue that acknowledgement of the political character of Genesis historically has been patchy. While, they suggest, some political elements have always been recognized within Genesis, those elements have been thought to be found only in later, redactional, text. The earlier layers have typically been understood to be legends or fairy tales (Gunkel), reliable historical reports (Albright) or old family stories (Westermann). Citing the work of Blum, however, Brett and Wöhrle (2018: 2) argue that 'The ancestral narratives are rather from the oldest literary kernels politically shaped.' My own experience has been that the resistance to recognizing Genesis as a political book has been strong. At the first meeting of the Society for Biblical Literature (SBL) that I attended I participated in a plenary discussion session in which the central question was 'Is Genesis a political book?' The session was well-attended and generated lively, even heated, discussion, but the conclusion expressed by the session chair was that we would probably never know the answer to the question. Things have changed markedly in the intervening ten to twelve years, however, and the chair of the session has been converted, becoming the author of one of the essays in *The Politics of the Ancestors*.

Undoubtedly, one of the reasons for resistance to viewing Genesis as a political book has been the domesticity of the setting for most of the stories. Childbirth is a core imperative from the first chapter, and this means that women, families and households are unusually prominent in Genesis. However, Genesis is a book that functions on multiple levels. Names given to several of the characters confirm that they represent not just themselves but nations as well. Most prominent among these, of course, is Jacob, who, in Gen. 32:29, is given the name 'Israel'. Lot is explicitly identified as the father (as well as grandfather!) of Israel's neighbours, Moab and Ammon, while

Esau is identified with Edom. In the latter chapters of Genesis, Jacob's twelve sons represent the twelve tribes of Israel and battle it out between themselves for preferment. Hagar's name (which means 'the alien' in Hebrew) presents her as the quintessential outsider. Abraham's name change in Genesis 17, meanwhile, is inherently political – instead of merely the 'father of many' (Abram), he becomes 'father of many peoples' (Abraham), and the etiological (i.e. explanatory) gloss in v.5 makes it clear that he is to be the progenitor of nations. It is arguable that by this move the Priestly writer expands Israel's vision for herself from one of nationhood to one of imperial aspiration. Arguably, too, the largely domestic setting of Genesis is significant in this regard, in assisting its political commentary and innovation to go under the radar. If a story is 'about' women and children and is set in the home, conventional thinking goes, then it is unlikely to be a story with great implications for matters of state.

'Political' readings tend, by their nature, to focus on the 'world behind the text'. They look to what is known about the political (and social, financial etc.) context of the time in which the text was likely composed or edited, and bring that knowledge to bear on questions about how the text functioned or functions. Typically, too, a reader adopting a political approach will be interested in the intention of the author – what was it that the author hoped to achieve by composing, or editing, or curating, this text? Brett and Wöhrle (2018: 3) write that the recent developments in historical-critical approach have been of 'major importance' for political interpretations of the ancestral narratives:

> While older research had to explain large parts of the ancestral narratives, and the political concepts implied by these texts, as stemming from the early monarchic times, recent approaches are able to explain these narratives in a more differentiated way. It is now possible to trace multi-levelled literary developments of the ancestral narratives, occurring over centuries – from the early monarchic period down to the later Persian times. This allows us to appreciate a multi-faceted history of the ever-new reflections upon the relationship between Israel and the neighbouring peoples.

I have written already in this guide about Genesis' extensive use of monarchic language and motifs, even suggesting that Abraham's story is structured on that of David. Given that the post-exilic dating of much, if not most, of the Abraham Cycle (at least among European scholars) means that the cycle comes from a time when there was no monarchy, and when hopes for a revival of the monarchy were being dashed, what might the purpose of retelling monarchic stories have been? I have argued elsewhere (Warner 2018a, 2023a) that, in the case of the Abraham Cycle, an editorial intention to depict a democratization of monarchic authority and responsibility is evident. In Gen. 18:17-19, and elsewhere, Abraham appears to have been appointed to the helm of a governance model in which the power and responsibility previously held by the king was transferred to a collective comprised of the (male) heads of Israelite households.

A different approach seems to be observable in the Joseph Story. The earliest layer of the 'novella' (which may well have been written during the monarchic period – opinions are divided, as discussed elsewhere in this guide) appears to have adopted the approach of modelling Joseph upon David for the purpose of promoting Joseph as a national hero of the north. It appears that in a later layer of the story, this modelling has been continued but inverted. Clues in the text suggest that a later (southern) layer depicts not Joseph but Judah as David. This later layer uses the story of the transfer of the monarchy from Saul to David as a model for a Joseph/Judah power tussle, suggesting that over the course of the story, the mantle of Jacob's pre-eminent son moves from Joseph to Judah, just as in the monarchic story kingly power moved from Saul to David (Warner 2023b).

A broad interpretation of what is 'political' expands the scope of a political approach. The examples I've offered so far have related to the politics of governance of a sovereign nation. 'Politics' may also refer to relationships and interactions between groups divided along ideological lines. So, for example, Brett (2000) has characterized Genesis as 'resistance literature' that opposes the exclusivist ideology and programme of Ezra and Nehemiah. Alternatively, it could be argued that Genesis is political in its presentation of a national origins story that competes with the origins story presented in Exodus. Politics may also be seen in a very general sense in a 'battle' or dialectic between Priestly and Deuteronomistic outlooks in which Genesis undoubtedly participates (Brett 2019).

Gen. 21:8-21

The political reading of Gen. 21:8-21 that I outline here builds on a reading of Brett (2000), as well as upon some aspects of the trauma-informed reading outlined above. Once again, the focus here is upon parallels between Sarah's demand that Abraham send away his Egyptian wife and child, Hagar and Ishmael, and the programme of Ezra in response to the 'foreign wives crisis' as outlined in Ezra 9–10.

One of the challenging elements of Ezra's exclusivist programme for today's readers is that the text does not offer anything by way of a clear underlying motivation. Ezra himself offers a loosely based objection to intermarriage grounded in purity concerns. He speaks of a mixing of the 'holy seed' (a concept not found elsewhere in the OT, except perhaps in Isa. 6:13) with 'the peoples of the lands'. Scholars exploring the text for explanations of Ezra's reportedly dramatic response to the issue of intermarriage have been able to identify possible motivations, all of a generally moralistic or theological nature, none of which have been accepted as a definitive reason for the instruction to expel foreign wives and children.

Gen. 21:8-21, on a political reading, steps into the debate, cutting through moralizing and theologizing, to expose inheritance concerns as the real reason behind Ezra's programme. Sarah's concern that Ishmael, the son of Abraham's Egyptian wife, should not inherit along with Isaac is offered as a representation of the reality that underlies Ezra's pious speech. Brett (2000: 61) puts it this way:

> If Sarah's complaint to Abraham in Gen 21.9-10 can be read as in some sense a political allegory of these events, then it is noticeable that the narrator has allowed Sarah's speech to render the driving away of a foreign woman in purely economic terms. There is no theological veneer to be found. Hagar and Ishmael's fate is determined solely by the question of inheritance. Interpreted in this way, the story is not primarily about Sarah as a vindictive woman; it is more generally about the politics of dispossession. Hagar's fate stands for the dispossession of many others who have inter-married, and if she is to be taken as exemplary then the name of her son indicates divine concern with all such suffering.

On Brett's reading, Gen. 21:8-21 is an 'under the radar' challenge to the hypocrisy of Ezra's programme, which it presents as financially self-serving.

I would like to add an additional observation to Brett's argument. In the trauma-informed reading of Gen. 21:8-21, above, I noted the prominence of Abraham's inner response to the 'intense evil' of Sarah's request of him. When that detail is brought to bear upon the argument forwarded by Brett, it can be suggested that Gen. 21:8-21 does more than expose the hypocrisy of Ezra's programme; it implicitly pronounces it 'exceedingly evil'. To give credence to Abraham's thoughts in this way, of course, shines a light on a theological problem in the text, which is that God explicitly condones this evil. Why would the Genesis authors wish to portray God as condoning evil? There is no easy answer to this question, except to observe that the theological problem is not isolated to this one story in Genesis. It is raised again in the very next chapter, Genesis 22, which opens with God's demand to Abraham that he slaughter Isaac. There are many parallels and connections between the two stories, Genesis 21 and 22, and this supports the idea that it is right to posit 'wrestling with issues of God's justice' as a motif of both of the stories of the threats to the lives of Abraham's sons.

Intersectionalist Readings

The two approaches addressed so far have had an historical bent. They have involved allowing what is known of the 'world behind the text' to inform reading of it. An intersectionalist approach is also cognizant of that world but expands its focus to draw in also the world 'in front of the text', and can be categorized as an 'ideological approach', in which the text is read through the lens of an ideological concern of the reader. Gale Yee (2018: 7) writes, 'The ideological criticisms investigate the power differentials in certain social relationships in the production of the text (who wrote it, when, and why), how these power relations in the text are reproduced in the text itself, and how they are consumed by readers of various social groups.'

Intersectionalism grew out of, and partly as a reaction to, feminism. There is a rich heritage of feminist readings of Genesis, and that heritage has been, in recent years, broadened and challenged by critical approaches emerging from it, such as womanism, ecofeminism, psychoanalytic feminism, socialist/Marxist feminisim, postcolonial feminism and numerous others. 'Intersectionality', a term coined in 1989 by Kimberlé Crenshaw, an African American lawyer, posits that power differentials are experienced differently, and simultaneously, by women in different contexts, and that power differentials caused by sex intersect in different contexts with power differentials caused by other elements, notably race and class. Feminist approaches have often been employed, argue intersectionalists, by white women living in relatively privileged contexts. The resulting readings may not reflect the experiences of Black or coloured women, or women of lower-class status. Meanwhile, Black scholarship done by Black men has tended to presume to speak for both Black men and women. Black women, intersectionalist scholars argue, are neither white women nor Black men, and so require approaches that can be sympathetic to a range of distinctions between marginalized groups. An intersectional reading is one in which the reader brings a range of power differentials together in a composite hermeneutical (i.e. interpretive) lens. Yee notes that intersectional reading had been happening long before the term was coined, albeit under other names, and that ideological concerns other than the classic foci of sex, race and class have been highlighted in intersectional readings, such as sexuality, colonial status, ethnicity and physical ability.

Genesis offers perhaps unusually fertile ground for intersectional reading, particularly in relation to the core categories of analysis of sex, race and class, because of its preoccupation with matters of identity and the categorization of people. Several of the female characters foregrounded in Genesis are women who also possess further characteristics of otherness. Among these, Hagar is a parade example – a woman whose fate is determined also by her Egyptian identity and her status as slave. In the narrative she is paired with, and pitted against, another woman, Sarah, whose Israelite identity and freewoman status grant her power over Hagar's life and body. In the Jacob Cycle, Bilhah and Zilpah function in a markedly similarly manner to Hagar, although without receiving the narrative attention given to her. In the Joseph Story, Tamar's race is not specified, but the context suggests that the reader may be intended to assume that she is non-Israelite and that her race, although not specified, is significant. Mrs Potiphar, meanwhile, is othered by her race even if she is presented as a woman of wealth and privilege. In addition, the text hints that her personal power is threatened also by her marriage to an infertile husband (the Hebrew word usually translated as 'officer' in Gen. 39:1 also means 'eunuch'). Fertility is also a factor that is highlighted in the presentation of the other women mentioned here. Unlike most of the Israelite women in Genesis, non-Israelite women are typically marked out by their fertility. Because of their other attributes, however, the fertility of these non-Israelite women tends to function as a goad as well as a resource for Israelite women characters, and it ultimately tends to become a factor that contributes to oppression.

Before looking at Gen. 21:8-21 through an intersectional lens, I would like to note one further feature of Genesis that such a lens reveals (but that is not highlighted in Genesis 21). Genesis participates in a trend, evidenced in other Old Testament books also, of presenting plurally disadvantaged women in quasi-heroic form. Tamar is perhaps the clearest example. As already noted, Tamar's ethnicity is implied rather than stated, but in her dealings she is paired with Judah, a privileged Israelite male who, having acquired her as wife for his eldest son, fails to do his Torah-duty towards her. In order to secure Judah's compliance with levirate marriage rules (see Deut. 25:5-10),

Tamar further 'others' herself by posing as a prostitute. Although her life is threatened, Judah eventually praises her righteousness, pronouncing it greater than his own. Tamar is listed by Matthew, in the genealogy opening his gospel, among a group of women othered by their race and smeared by innuendo of sexual misconduct but who exhibited righteousness in their pursuit of Israelite survival. Given numerous parallels between Tamar's story and the story of the Daughters of Lot (and mothers of Ammon and Moab) in Gen. 19:30-38, it is arguable that Lot's Daughters are presented in analogous manner, despite the fact that most commentators (very often male) have focused on their 'shame'. (The editors of some editions of the NRSV have inserted the heading 'The Shameful Origin of Moab and Ammon'.) Hagar, too, could be considered one of these heroines, even if her heroism consists largely in surviving oppression. The presentation of Hagar in Genesis is quite extraordinary. This foreign slave women is the central character of two full chapters of the Abraham Cycle; she is the only character in the OT to 'name' God (Gen. 16:13), with whom she converses face to face, as Abraham does (but Sarah does not), and she receives divine promises in respect of her son that are never conferred upon Isaac. My reason for pointing out this trend is to highlight the fact that it is precisely in the intersection of power imbalances that the women in question are identified. It is crucial to their presentation that they are not merely women but also non-Israelite and compromised also for additional reasons, such as class or sexual suspicion.

Gen. 21:8-21

An intersectional reading is likely to pay attention to elements of the narrative that other readings have passed over. The two earlier readings, for example, have had little use for consideration of Hagar, except to the extent that she is representative of the category 'foreign wife and mother', who must, pursuant to Ezra's programme, be removed. I was even able to stop half-way in my brief introduction to the story, because neither reading approach paid great attention to the details of the narrative between Hagar's expulsion and her salvation at God's hands. For an intersectionalist reader, conversely, Hagar is a rich character, who experiences power differentials in each of the three classic categories, sex, race and class. The reader need not end their exploration with these three classic categories, however. Delores S. Williams (2006: 177) writes, 'A careful reading of Genesis 16:1-16 and Genesis 21:9-21 reveals that Hagar's predicament involved slavery, poverty, ethnicity, sexual and economic exploitation, surrogacy, domestic violence, homelessness, single parenting, and radical encounters with God.' Williams further suggests that 'African American women's historic predicament in society resembles Hagar's in the biblical story'. Williams, who identifies her approach as 'womanist' (a term coined by Alice Walker to designate the work of a Black feminist or a feminist of colour, and which is typically adopted by African American scholars), is interested in how, and why, African American women appropriate the stories of Hagar. Her reading of the two Hagar stories, in Genesis 16 and 21, disabuses her of the idea that Hagar's story could be helpfully considered one of 'liberation':

> It was obvious to me that God's response to Hagar in Genesis was not liberation. Rather, God participated in Hagar and her child's survival on many occasions. When she was a runaway slave, God met her in the wilderness and told her to return to Sarai and Abram's domicile. Then, when Hagar and her child were finally cast out of the home of their oppressors and were not given proper resources for survival, God provided Hagar with a resource. She received new vision to see survival resources where she had seen none before. Thus it seems to me that God's response to Hagar's (and her child's) situation was survival and involvement in their development of a quality of life appropriate to their situation and their heritage (e.g. Gen. 21:20).

Williams observes that many African American women believe that God has directly assisted them also in situations that seemed to lack any prospect for survival, or which seemed to offer no potential quality of life. She suggests that the female-centred tradition of appropriation of Bible stories that she observes might usefully be named 'the survival, quality of life tradition' of African American biblical appropriation. 'In Black consciousness', she concludes, 'God's survival and quality of life response to Hagar is God's response to survival and quality of life to African American women and mothers of slave descent struggling to sustain their families with God's help'.

Williams' is, of course, just one intersectionalist response to the Hagar story (or stories), but it illustrates at least two important aspects of intersectional reading. First, it points to an assumed imperative to build connections between biblical stories and traditions and the lived lives of women labouring under a given intersection of power imbalances that is close to the heart of the reader. Second, it is a *theological* reading, with a strong focus on practical application, pointing to the significance of theological insight as well as its application to lived experience.

Ecological Readings

Genesis has occupied a special place in the history of ecological approaches to reading biblical text. This is unsurprising, given its creation focus. The field was born through challenge. Lynn White, in a highly influential article published in *Science*, 'The Historical Root of our Ecological Crisis' (1967), laid much of the blame for our perilous ecological state at the feet of biblical tradition and its reception, with Genesis as a particular target. He accused the creation accounts of irredeemable anthropocentrism:

> By gradual stages a loving and all-powerful God had created light and darkness, the heavenly bodies, the earth and all its plants, animals, birds, and fishes. Finally, God had created Adam and, as an afterthought, Eve to keep man from being lonely. Man [note that White is writing in 1967!] named all the animals, thus establishing his dominance over them. God planned all of this explicitly for man's benefit and rule: no item in the physical creation had any purpose save to serve man's purposes. And, although man's body is made of clay, he is not simply part of nature: he is made in God's image.

In conclusion, White delivered his opinion that 'Especially in its Western form, Christianity is the most anthropocentric religion the world has seen'. It is arguable that White's is a poor reading of the text, and indeed this has been argued eloquently. Ellen F. Davis (2007: 83), for example, has since written of 'the biblical view that there is an unbreakable three-way connection between people, God and land' and M. Gene Tucker (1997: 8) of 'the integral relationship of humanity to the [natural] world'. Mbuvi's kinship approach (2016) appeals to the genealogical structure of Genesis, and Earth's key position in that structure, to challenge allegations of anthropocentrism. Rightly, in my view, she points to Gen. 2:5 as indicating that 'humans partner with God in nurturing the land, and are nurtured by it in return' (2016: 51). As Mbuvi suggests (building on the work of Theodore Hiebert), Genesis 2 opens with a presenting narrative issue – the Earth lacks water and creatures to serve it. The focus is not upon humans, or some human lack, but upon Earth and what Earth lacks. This presenting lack becomes the prompt for God to bring rain and to create humans to 'serve' Earth (Gen. 2:5, 15). All of this being said, nevertheless, White's article was an important challenge, and White was only presenting a view that most ordinary readers at the time, and probably also the majority of scholars, accepted or even took for granted.

In the intervening years 'ecological' or 'green' hermeneutics have blossomed (no pun intended), and Genesis has continued to be a key focus. Not only have individual scholars adopted these hermeneutics but a number of larger 'projects' have been mounted to build hermeneutical frameworks for ecological reading of biblical texts. Two, in particular, deserve mention. The first, 'The Earth Bible Project' emanated from Australia, where it was spearheaded by Norman C. Habel. This project set out to interrogate both the biblical text and its reception by proposing six 'eco-justice' lenses for reading text:

1. The principle of intrinsic worth: The universe, Earth and all its components have intrinsic worth/value.
2. The principle of interconnectedness: Earth is a community of interconnected living things that are mutually dependent on each other for life and survival.
3. The principle of voice: Earth is a subject capable of raising its voice in celebration and against injustice.
4. The principle of purpose: The universe, Earth and all its components are part of a dynamic cosmic design within which each piece has a place in the overall goal of that design.
5. The principle of mutual custodianship: Earth is a balanced and diverse domain where responsible custodians can function as partners with, rather than rulers over, Earth to sustain its balance and a diverse Earth community.
6. The principle of resistance: Earth and its components not only suffer from human injustices but actively resist them in the struggle for justice. (Trudinger and Habel 2008)

Readings presented under the umbrella of the Earth Bible Project have adopted a number of distinctive approaches, including distinguishing between 'green' and 'grey' biblical text and, in the application of lens three, ascribing a voice to Earth, even to the extent of furnishing Earth with speeches. (In this study guide I have adopted the Project's approach of capitalizing the first letter of Earth's name.)

A second project has been undertaken in England, by a team based at Exeter University and headed by David G. Horrell. The Exeter Group seeks to situate its approach between that of the Earth Bible Project and those scholars whose work they view as tending towards the excessively apologetic, presenting recovery exercises that can gloss over some of the more difficult aspects of the text. On the other hand, the Exeter Group takes the view that the approach of the Earth Bible Project can tend too much towards a hermeneutic of suspicion, leaning readily towards conclusions that the biblical text is inconvenient, ambivalent and sometimes damaging. The Exeter Group seeks to position itself somewhere in between the two poles and it, too, proposes lenses for ecological hermeneutics, although developed from what they see as biblical themes and concepts, in contrast to the non-biblically sourced 'eco-justice principles' adopted by the Earth Bible Project. The Exeter Group lenses include the following:

- the goodness of all creation, humanity as part of the community of creation;
- interconnectedness in failure and flourishing;
- the covenant with all creation;
- creation's calling to praise God; and
- liberation and reconciliation for all things. (Horrell 2014)

Gen. 21:8-21

An ecological hermeneutic is not an obvious approach to reading Gen. 21:8-21. In this it is unlike the intersectionalist approach explored above, to which Gen. 21:8-21 lends itself richly. Nevertheless, reading Gen. 21:8-21 through an ecological or 'green' lens draws out meaning from the story that is likely lost in other approaches, and at least one scholar, Laura Hobgood-Oster, has attempted such a reading. Hobgood-Oster's reading appears in an Earth Bible Project collection of essays titled *The Earth Story in Genesis* (2000). It is part of an essay that focuses on the (surprisingly) many instances of wells in Genesis narratives. One of its stated aims is to make the wells of Genesis 'characters'.

Wells feature in many types of stories in Genesis. As Alter (1981) noted, wells are elements of type scenes in which, for example, the hero meets a woman, or a character encounters the divine. The latter occurs in Gen. 21:8-21. After Hagar and Ishmael have been banished, they wander in the wilderness until their meagre supplies of water have been exhausted. Hagar sits the two of them down and prepares to die, weeping. God hears her voice and the 'angel of God' speaks to her, repeating the promise to make of Ishmael a great nation. God opens Hagar's eyes and she sees a well – precisely the thing she needs for the survival of herself and her son.

In her reading, Hobgood-Oster describes the opening of Hagar's eyes, allowing her to see the well, as 'one of the most powerful acts of justice presented in Genesis'. Referencing the two Hagar stories, Genesis 16 and 21:8-21, she writes (2000: 194):

> In both of these stories, wells provide life-giving water for the most oppressed, the slaves, the banished ones. Though they could be perceived as a threat to the promise of God to Abram and Sarai, therefore as outsiders less deserving of the love of the divine, Earth again acts with justice. As wells are revealed, eco-justice takes place and wells are revealed to all, regardless of falsely-perceived status or culturally assigned worth.

Hobgood-Oster offers as an additional insight into the observation that in the story the human had to have her eyes opened by God before she was able to perceive the well, suggesting that God must open our eyes to the power of nature. The well, the story implies, exists. The human character just couldn't see it. Hobgood-Oster suggests a further question: 'Do the oppressors block the view of the oppressed by reserving the resources for themselves? Only when ecojustice principles challenge the powerful ones who claim earth's resources will the banished ones have access to the wells.' Although Hobgood-Oster doesn't note it, the very next pericope (Gen. 21:22-34) tells of negotiations over a well between 'powerful ones', Abraham and King Abimelech.

I'd like to add an observation that addresses justice *to* Earth to Hobgood Oster's reading, with its emphasis on justice *of* Earth. In the story, the human characters share a presupposition about Earth – wrongly as it happens. In the story the movement of the characters is from 'civilization' (Abraham and Sarah's camp) towards 'wilderness'. The presupposition of all the characters is that 'wilderness' is a place of lack and, ultimately, of death. One must take supplies if one is to venture there without risking one's life. In fact, one of the 'shock' elements of the story is that the supplies Abraham gives to Hagar are too meagre to be likely to hold off death for long. Death, however, does not occur. The water that is so crucial to life is there in the wilderness. Hagar just needs, as Hobgood-Oster notes, her eyes to be opened in order to be able to perceive it. In the final verse of the pericope we learn that Ishmael continues 'to live' (or 'dwell') in 'the wilderness of Paran' with his mother. Part of the witness of the story is that humans can mistakenly characterize parts of Earth that have not been subjected to human 'civilization' as places of death. God is needed to open the eyes of humans to recognize that life exists apart from and beyond parts of Earth that humans have adapted to their use.

Intertextual Readings

Intertextuality, as an approach to biblical interpretation, is both ancient and new. The idea that texts interpret one another is central to the very earliest biblical reading, yet 'intertextuality' was not coined as a term prior to the work of Julia Kristeva in the late twentieth century. This short introduction will focus on newer, or 'second wave', approaches.

Kristeva wrote, 'Any text is constructed as a mosaic of quotations; any text is the absorption and transformation of another' (1980: 66). Marianne Grohmann and Hyun Chul Paul Kim (2019: 1) add:

> any reader too is a byproduct of a mosaic of cultural traditions, social contexts, and ideological concepts. Put together, both texts and readers share intricate, interactive interconnections in the webs of mutual and multifaceted influences. Texts are constructed in dialogues whether intentionally/uniquely or unintentionally/universally. Readers, too, engage in understanding the texts in light of numerous other readers, be they ancient authors/readers, contemporary readers, and even future readers. How such is the case and what we the interpreters can make out of it have been groundbreaking and rewarding outcomes of the theory of intertextuality.

One of the fascinating features of intertextuality is its drawing together of all three interpretive 'worlds'. One might initially imagine that intertextuality lives most naturally in the 'world of the text' – that the task in which one is engaged when adopting intertextuality as an approach is that of reading of two or more texts together for the purpose of enquiring as to the meaning that is drawn out of a text through its engagement with another/others. When phrased in this manner, the focus is on the text, or, rather, texts, and their dialogue. Yet, as the above quote from Grohmann and Kim suggests, the role of the reader, too, and the multiplicity of what the reader brings to the activity of reading, is central to a Kristevan intertextuality, so that intertextuality is properly understood also as a 'world in front of the text' approach to interpretation. To push this idea a step further, intertextuality is properly characterized as an ideological approach that maintains a focus on questions of 'power' to no lesser an extent than the intersectional and ecological hermeneutical approaches discussed above. Intertextuality, as an approach, takes power from the author (the idea that a text means what its author intended it to mean) and locates it instead in the reader (the idea that the text means what it comes to mean in the dialogue between text and reader). Grohmann and Kim (2019: 4) write, 'Put simply, the reader is no longer an inferior slave to the authoritative text but rather an emancipated, empowered and equal co-producer, deliverer or even re-presenter.' Yet even this emphasis on the power of the reader (and the associated idea of 'the death of the author') should not eclipse entirely the extent to which intertextuality engages, or may engage, the world 'behind the text'. Kristeva's concept of intertextuality embraces such approaches as the burgeoning field of 'inner-biblical exegesis', in which biblical texts are read together for a range of purposes, which may include enquiry as to authorial intention, the direction and scope of dependence between texts (on this issue see further below), and the contexts (historical, political, social etc.) in which texts were composed, edited or curated. Indeed, the role of contexts in intertextuality should not be underestimated, so that intertextuality can properly be seen as an exercise in which ancient and contemporary contexts are brought into conversation.

In the decades since Kristeva coined the term 'intertextuality', it has grown rapidly as an approach, and come to mean many more things than its 'author' might have intended or imagined, to the extent that it becomes difficult to say what is included under the umbrella of intertextuality and what is better considered to be outside it. Further, intertextuality has lent itself to combined application with other approaches. Each of the readings of Gen. 21:8-21 offered here, for example, has engaged intertextuality alongside the specified approach. The trauma-informed and political readings appealed to biblical accounts of post-return Judah and particularly those of Ezra and Nehemiah. Meanwhile, very few intersectional readers would approach the passage without recourse also to the parallel Hagar story in Genesis 16, while Hobgood-Oster's reading was offered in the context of a study of textual references to wells throughout Genesis.

A core issue in determining the scope of intertextuality as an approach has been that of 'dependence'. Is intertextuality interested only in texts that can properly be said to be dependent upon one another, that is, where an author (whether intentionally or unintentionally) depended upon, or was influenced by, one of the partner texts in the process of composing or editing the other? Alternatively, has ideology about the relative power of author and reader meant that intertextuality has embraced only the study of dialogue between texts that can be considered free of the creative intention of the authors or editors of the texts? In true post-modern style, intertextual method has come to be seen to embrace both.

For the purpose of organizing their discussion, and the essays included in their 2019 collection, Grohmann and Kim suggest two categories (2019: 13):

- **i** 'Inner-Biblical Intertextuality (within the canonical corpus of the Hebrew Bible)'; and
- **ii** 'Postbiblical Intertextuality (outside the Hebrew Bible)'.

The former category includes the reading of texts both for the purpose of assessing dependence between them (or the reliance or intention of the author[s] of the texts) and in circumstances in which the reader assumes there to be no dependence (whether intentional or unintentional) between them (i.e. where there is no basis for assuming that the author(s) of either of the texts knew, or had ever encountered, the other). The latter category, similarly, includes the reading of texts both for the purposes of assessing dependence between biblical and postbiblical texts and in circumstances in which the reader assumes there to be no dependence (whether intentional or unintentional) between them whatsoever. Even in this latter case, intertextuality claims, the two texts may fruitfully be in dialogue, both with each other and with their readers.

Gen. 21:8-21

Inner-Biblical Intertextuality

I have already observed that each of the four readings of Gen. 21:8-21, above, has engaged an inner-biblical approach to some degree or another. There are further important inner-biblical intertexts that have not yet been mentioned or barely so. One of those is the New Testament book Galatians, and its reception and treatment of the Hagar and Sarah tradition. Another is the story of the threat to the life of Isaac in Gen. 22:1-19. Scholars have identified a very large number of similarities and parallels between the two stories, to the extent that perhaps no reading of Gen. 21:8-21 can claim to be comprehensive without at least some reference to Gen. 22:1-19, and vice-versa. For example, appeal to Gen. 22:1-19 has the capacity to enrich and inform each of the readings already offered. So, bringing the Isaac and Ishmael stories into dialogue in a trauma-informed reading, and observing Abraham's lack of emotional, moral or other inner response to the divine directive to slaughter Isaac, may serve further to emphasize Abraham's emotional response to Sarah's demand that he expel Ishmael, and therefore to reassure a reader required to expel his own foreign wife and son that his emotional and moral responses are both natural and authorized. In a political reading, recourse to Gen. 22:1-19 may make the point that the divine promise are repeated to Abraham not following his expulsion of Ishmael (in line with the Ezra programme) but after Abraham's successful passing of an altogether different kind of test (Gen. 22:15-18). Meanwhile, in an intersectional reading, one might note with interest the fact that Hagar's prominence in Gen. 21:8-21, even if less marked than that in Genesis 16, nevertheless eclipses that of Sarah in Gen. 22:1-19, who is excluded entirely from the story of the threat to the life of her own son. Finally, in an ecological reading, a reader might note the parallel that in both stories the child is saved once his parent's eyes are opened (or lifted) to elements of the natural world – a well in the case of Gen. 22:19 and a ram in Gen. 22:13.

It is important to add here that inner-biblical exegesis (or as Nihan [2007] has suggested, 'inner-legal exegesis') is a crucial tool for exposing the implicit, but nevertheless extensive, dialogue between Genesis and Torah. Gen. 26:5 may be the only place in which the explicit language of Torah is permitted to penetrate Genesis narrative, but implicit engagement and dialogue with Torah permeates Genesis. Brief mention of an example related to Gen. 21:8-21 must suffice. I have argued elsewhere (Warner 2018b) that Gen. 21:8-21 can fruitfully be read in dialogue with the inheritance legislation of Deut. 21:15-17 (and with Gen. 29:18, 33; 48:22 and 49:3, which also dialogue with these verses from Deuteronomy). The insights of such an intertextual reading inform richly the political and intersectional readings of Gen. 21:8-21 outlined above. Inner-biblical exegesis, additionally, with its relational focus, seems to be offering a fruitful way forward through the impasse currently afflicting historical-critical method.

Postbiblical Intertextuality

In her 2020 book, *Writing and Reading to Survive: Biblical and Contemporary Trauma Narratives in Conversation*, L. Juliana M. Claassens touches on all of these hermeneutical approaches in a collection of essays having their primary focus on postbiblical intertextuality. In one of the included essays, 'Handmaids' Tales', she reads the stories of Rachel, Leah, Bilhah and Zilpah (Genesis 29–35) together with Margaret Atwood's *The Handmaid's Tale* (1986). This is an example of a postbiblical intertextual reading in which the dependence of the postbiblical text upon the biblical text not only is assumed but has been extensively addressed by the author in articles and interviews. (Of course, given the profound impact of biblical tradition upon Western culture, at least, one might question whether any Western postbiblical literature could be assumed to have no dependence upon biblical text.) Atwood based her novel on the story of the mothers of Jacob's children (and thus of the Tribes of Israel), but the parallels between those stories and that of Hagar and Ishmael are strong, and Claassens refers to Gen. 21:8-21 in her discussion. For example, she notes (2020: 79) that 'The disdain shown to Sarah by a pregnant Hagar can be seen reflected in the disdain with which June is treated by the Commander's wife Serena Joy, who responds with contempt to Offred's presence in her house.'

Despite the fact that Attwood's novel takes as its inspiration the stories of Jacob's wives (and of the surrogacy arrangements through which some of his children are born), rather than those of Abraham's wives (and Hagar's role as surrogate), there is a further striking parallel between the novel and Gen. 21:8-21 (which is not reflected in Genesis 29–35). In Atwood's dystopian society 'Gilead', handmaids (surrogates) who did not prove successful in producing children for commanders and their wives within a stipulated time period were 'sent away' to 'the Colonies' – areas that had been contaminated by pollution and radioactive waste. Although officially this was a matter of re-assignment to a different form of work (dealing with the pollution and waste), in reality it was assumed that being sent to the Colonies was a form of death sentence, just as it is assumed by all of the characters in Gen. 21:8-21 that Hagar's expulsion would lead to the deaths of herself and her son.

What is the value of reading biblical text in conversation with other texts written later? How can dialogue with subsequent literature help in the quest to draw meaning *from* biblical text (exegesis) rather than, say, risk the worst consequences of reading meaning *into* biblical text (eisegesis)? (The question whether there is, in fact, any real difference between these two things is complex, and beyond the scope of this study guide.) There are, of course, many answers to these questions. One of the more chilling aspects of *The Handmaid's Tale* is its depiction of a society which, although based on Genesis and elements of the theologies and ideologies of Genesis, pushes those theologies and ideologies, and their potential practical application, to gruesome extremes, so that elements of Genesis that might be assumed to be theologically wholesome, or at least benign, such as the centrality of Genesis' emphasis on human procreation, are demonstrated to have the capacity, when pushed to extremes, to function in malignant fashion. In this respect, a novel can demonstrate to postmodern readers the possible implications of biblical stories and traditions when de-contextualized, which of course is something that happens regularly in today's world. Indeed, the capacity of contemporary literature to bring biblical narratives into contemporary discourse and to impact current events is something addressed by Claassens and by Atwood herself. The Handmaid's Tale is a particularly fascinating example text in this respect. It's 'bringing forward' of biblical narrative into the author's own time proved to speak cogently not only into that time but to the later period of Trumpian United States, to the extent that the author was moved to write a sequel, inspired by the parallels between that later time and the dystopian society imagined in the first novel. Claassens (2020: 95) quotes Michiko Kakutani:

> How did the United States of America become the totalitarian state of Gilead – a place where women are treated as 'two-legged wombs'; where nonwhite residents and unbelievers (that is, Jews, Catholic, Quakers, Baptists, anyone who does not embrace the fundamentalist extremism of Gilead) are resettled, exiled or disappeared; where leadership deliberately uses gender, race and class to divide the country?

A discussion of intertextual approaches, with their capacity to draw in, and to function alongside, other hermeneutical approaches, seems a good place at which to end this chapter, with its all-too-brief and all-too-limited introductions to a range of recent approaches to reading, and drawing meaning from, Genesis. Indeed, it seems, too, a good place at which to end this all-too-brief (some readers may disagree …) and all-too-limited Study Guide to Genesis. As author, I can hope only to have whet the appetites of readers to learn more about the extraordinary book of Genesis. Just as Atwood's novel spoke not only to the generation of its earliest audience but also to the generations that followed, so does the 'past' offered by Genesis to its first audiences, desperately in need of a future, speak to audiences today, for whom also the need for a 'future' can seem, all too often, both urgent and pressing.

References

Alter, Robert. (1981), *The Art of Biblical Narrative*, New York: Basic Books.

Atwood, Margaret. (1986), *The Handmaid's Tale*, Boston, MA: Houghton Miffler Harcourt.

Boase, Elizabeth and Christopher Frechette (eds). (2016). *Bible through the Lens of Trauma*, SBLSS 86, Atlanta, GA: SBL Press.

Brett, Mark G. (2000), *Genesis: Procreation and the Politics of Identity*, OTR, London: Routledge.

Brett, Mark G. (2019), *Locations of God: Political Theology in the Hebrew Bible*, Oxford: Oxford University Press.

Brett, Mark G. and Jakob Wöhrle (eds). (2018). *Politics of the Ancestors: Exegetical and Historical Perspectives on Genesis 12–36*, FAT 124, Tübingen: Mohr Siebeck.

Carr, David M. (2014), *Holy Resilience: The Bible's Traumatic Origins*, New Haven: Yale University Press.

Claassens, L. Juliana M. (2020), *Writing and Reading to Survive: Biblical and Contemporary Trauma Narratives in Conversation*, BMW 74, TB 1, Sheffield: Sheffield Phoenix Press.

Davis, Ellen F. (2007), 'Propriety and Trespass: The Drama of Eating', *Ex Auditu* 23: 74–86.

Grohmann, Marianne and Hyun Chul Paul Kim (eds). (2019), *Second Wave Intertextuality and the Hebrew Bible*, SBLRBS 93, Atlanta, GA: SBL Press.

Habel, Norman C. and Peter Trudinger (eds). (2008), *Exploring Ecological Hermeneutics*, SBLSymp 46, Atlanta, GA: SBL Press.

Hendel, Ronald (ed.). (2010), *Reading Genesis: Ten Methods*, Cambridge: Cambridge University Press.

Hobgood-Oster, Laura. (2000), '"For out of That Well the Flocks Were Watered": Stories of Wells in Genesis', in Norman C. Habel and Shirley Wurst (eds), *The Earth Story in Genesis*, 187–99, Sheffield: Sheffield Academic.

Horrell, David. (2014), 'Ecological Hermeneutics: Reflections on Methods and Prospects for the Future', *Colloquium* 46(2): 166–9.

Kristeva, Julia. (1980), *Desire in Language: A Semiotic Approach to Literature and Art*, New York: Columbia University Press.

Mbuvi, Amanda Beckenstein. (2016), *Belonging in Genesis: Biblical Israel and the Politics of Identity Formation*, Waco, TX: Baylor.

Nihan, Christophe. (2007), *From Priestly Torah to Pentateuch*, FAT II 25, Tübingen: Mohr Siebeck.

O'Connor, Kathleen M. (2018), *Genesis 1–25A*, Macon, GA: Smyth & Helwys.

O'Connor, Kathleen M. (2020), *Genesis 25B–50*, Macon, GA: Smyth & Helwys.

Tucker, Gene M. (1997), 'Rain on a Land Where No One Lives: The Hebrew Bible on the Environment', *JBL* 116(1): 3–17.

Warner, Megan. (2018a), *Re-Imagining Abraham: A Re-Assessment of the Influence of Deuteronomism in Genesis*, OTS 72, Leiden: Brill.

Warner, Megan. (2018b), 'What If They're Foreign?: Inner-Legal Exegesis in the Ancestral Narratives', in Mark G. Brett and Jakob Wöhrle (eds), *The Politics of the Ancestors: Exegetical and Historical Perspectives on Genesis 12–36*, 67–92, FAT 124, Tübingen: Moher Siebeck.

Warner, Megan. (2023a), '"My Steadfast, Sure Love for David": Abraham and the World-View of Deutero-Isaiah', in Anja Marshall and Andreas Schüle (eds), *Exodus und Erzeltern in Deuterojesaja*, 49–63, Leipzig: Evangelische Verlagsanstalt.

Warner, Megan. (2023b), '"Are You Indeed to Reign over Us?": The Politics of Genesis 37–50', in Mark G. Brett and Rachelle Gilmour (eds), *Political Theologies in the Hebrew Bible*, 193–206, JAJ Sup, Leiden: Brill.

White, Lynn Jr. (1967), 'The Historic Roots of Our Ecologic Crisis', *Science* 155(3767): 1203–7.

Williams, Delores S. (2006), 'Hagar in African American Biblical Appropriation', in Phyllis Trible and Letty M. Russell (eds), *Hagar, Sarah, and Their Children: Jewish, Christian and Muslim Perspectives*, 171–84, Louisville, KY: Westminster John Knox Press.

Yee, Gale A. (2018), *The Hebrew Bible: Feminist and Intersectional Perspectives*, Minneapolis, MN: Fortress Press.

Index of Names

Index of Subjects

Index of References